Contents

Acknowledgements

We would like to thank the following people for kindly
contributing material from their own collections for inclusion
in this catalogue, thereby adding to its diversity;

 Jean Alexander
 Andy Myers
 Chris Stamper
 Steven Morgan-Vandome
 Philip Harrison
 David Robinson
 A. Delicata
 Bob Wilcock
 Roger Unsworth.

We would also like to thank the following for their kind
assistance;

 Royal Mail Stamps and Collectibles
 Allan Grant, Rushstamps
 Paul Dauwalder, Dauwalders
 Hugh Jefferies, Stanley Gibbons
and, most of all, Michael Morse whose knowledge of
presentation packs proved invaluable throughout the
production of this catalogue.

In addition, we are grateful to the British Postal Museum
and the Royal Philatelic Society London for the use of their
resources.

A Packs & Cards Catalogue of
British Stamp Presentation Packs

...TATION PACKS

First Edition

PACKS & CARDS

Oaklands House, Reading Road North
Fleet, Hants, GU51 4AB, England

Tel: +44 (0)1252 360530
info@PacksAndCards.com
www.PresentationPacks.com

Published by Packs & Cards (Traffic Names Ltd)
Oaklands House, Reading Road North,
Fleet, Hants, GU51 4AB, England

ISBN-13: 978-0-9928675-0-8

Printed by Polestar Wheatons, Exeter

Foreword

Hello and a very warm welcome to the first ever catalogue of British Stamp Presentation Packs.

Royal Mail has been producing and publishing these wonderful packs for over 50 years, so it seemed like the perfect time to produce this guide. Personally, I have been interested in British stamps for nearly 40 years, having started trading with my school friends in my teens. There were no mobile phones, tablets, or even calculators back then and stamp collecting was already a very popular hobby. In 1978, this growing interest led me to become a sole trader.

Over the years, collecting trends have evolved and the profile of collectors has changed to the point where it is not deemed critical to collect 'one of everything' but perhaps collect around a theme, such as 'people' or 'places of interest'. I like to refer to presentation packs as 'collectible memories', which encapsulates the moment in time that they represent.

Presentation packs, as opposed to just the stamps, have emerged to be one of the most popular and interesting collecting areas of philately. Presentation packs not only retain the mint, usable, stamps as issued, they also feature wonderful images and are packed with interesting information.

Many years of experience and man-hours have gone into the production of this catalogue. Consideration has been given to the categorisation, descriptions, numbering system, format and many other aspects. Our objectives have been to:
1. Make it easy to use
2. Have depth of detail for the specialist collector
3. Be informative and interesting

This first edition may not be perfect, but we have done our best to achieve these objectives.

I would like to thank the fantastic staff at Packs & Cards for all their hard work, all the contributors and mostly you for buying this catalogue. I hope you find it as fascinating and illuminating to read as we have found it to compile.

I wish you great pleasure and enjoyment in building your presentation pack collection.

Best regards

Ian Andrew

Ian Andrew
Catalogue Editor and Founder of Packs & Cards

Written and produced by Helen Owen
Design concept by Jody Jones
Researched and co-edited by Dr Amanda Grieve

Introduction

This catalogue is designed to categorise, list and illustrate the 1,000+ presentation packs that the Royal Mail has published since 1960, when it experimented with the first ever British Stamp Presentation Packs, known as Forerunners.

At the time, Royal Mail was known as the General Post Office (GPO) and had been since 1660 when it was established by Charles II. It wasn't until the Post Office Act of 1969 that the GPO was changed to a statutory corporation known simply as the Post Office.

The Post Office became a Public Limited Company in 2000 and was renamed Consignia plc in 2001. The new name was intended to show that the company did more than deliver mail, however, the change was very unpopular with both the public and employees and the following year it was announced that the company would be renamed Royal Mail Group plc.

With the exception of Private Packs, the packs listed herein contain Royal Mail mint stamps and were produced by Royal Mail. The section of Souvenir and Special Edition Packs includes some that, whilst still produced by Royal Mail, might have been distributed by third parties.

The vast array of designs, formats, shapes, content and sizes of presentation packs has meant that categorising them has been no easy task. We believe, however, that we have produced a catalogue which clearly lays out the packs in a logical, and chronological, format within clearly defined sections.

The most populated section is that of Commemorative Packs, which are listed first. These are the most recognisable and consistent in size and format, which makes them a great starting point to build a collection. These packs comprise a set of commemorative Royal

Mail mint stamps, held on a Hagner-type black card, encompassed by an information card (the most important element) and all contained within a clear plastic sleeve.

The listed prices are in pound sterling. They are a guide to the price you might expect to pay for each item in good, clean, undamaged condition. These are current at the time of publication (April 2014).

Whilst we have exhausted our knowledge of existing packs, we recognise that there could be some in circulation of which we aren't aware. We welcome submissions and suggestions for inclusion in future editions of this catalogue.

Pack numbering

This catalogue uses 'PP' (Presentation Packs) as a prefix to the catalogue numbers used within. For reference, we have also included Royal Mail printed pack numbers in the listings.

The PP numbering system is designed to be simple, clear and thorough.

The PP prefixes are as follows:
Commemorative Packs - PP
Definitive Packs - PPD
Collectors Club Packs - PPC
Forerunner Packs - PPF
Greetings Packs - PPG
Miniature Sheet Collection Packs - PPM
Postage Due Packs - PPT
Post & Go Packs - PPP
Reproduction Packs - PPR
Smilers for Kids Packs - PPS
Year Packs - PPYP
Year Books - PPYB

The sections on Format Packs, Souvenir and Special Editions, and Private Packs are not numbered as there are likely to be items in circulation beyond those listed.

Royal Mail numbering

It did not prove logical for us to use the Royal Mail pack numbers for several reasons. The Royal Mail numbering;
- did not start at the beginning
- did not appear on the packs for a period of years
- was omitted from time to time
- doubled-up occasionally
- had two systems running simultaneously for Commemorative and Definitive Packs
- introduced additional prefixes

The 1968 British Paintings Commemorative Pack (PP22) was the first that Royal Mail referred to with a number i.e pack 1, but it was not until the 1969 Christmas pack (PP30) that the number was included as part of the design and printed on the back of the pack. The same sequence of numbers was used for the Commemorative, Definitive and Year Packs. This appears to have led to a few mistakes and there are examples of number duplication, leading to some requiring an 'A' or 'B' suffix.

In 1983, a separate numbering system was introduced for the Definitive and Country Packs, but there has never been a pack numbered '16'. It is unknown whether this was due to a withdrawal, or if the number was accidently omitted.

Due to the production of additional packs in celebration of special events, such as Royal Weddings and British sporting successes, a special numbering system, known as the 'M' series, was created and applied. This series started with the Commemorative Pack for the Royal Wedding of Prince Edward and Sophie Rhys Jones, which is printed pack number M01. However, there are some anomalies in the M series, with the 2003 Rugby World Cup Winners Commemorative Pack labelled M9B, and there are two packs printed with M10; the 2004 Occasions pack and the 2005 Royal Wedding pack.

History and development of presentation packs

The first presentation packs were issued by the General Post Office (GPO) in 1960, when they were looking for a convenient way of packaging and selling sets of stamps for the London 1960 International Stamp Exhibition, held at the Royal Festival Hall. They produced four packs priced in pound sterling for the exhibition, and another four priced in US dollars for a Post Office sales tour of the USA. Each pack was fairly basic in design; the stamps were mounted on blue-grey card and enclosed in a paper envelope with a clear plastic window. The only information printed on the packs was a brief description of the stamps and the retail price. These presentation packs were produced in very limited numbers and are now known as Forerunners.

It was in 1964 that the first Commemorative Packs were produced by the GPO. On 23rd April, the first 'proper' pack was issued for a set of stamps celebrating the Shakespeare Festival, which marked the 400th Anniversary of William Shakespeare's birth. The presentation pack was decorative in design and contained information on the stamp designs, the designer and stamp printer. The pack was available to buy from the Philatelic Bureau and at Post Offices, as well as at a travelling exhibit sent to Head Postmasters around the country, which had been devised to promote the stamps and the Festival. The launch of the Shakespeare pack was very successful, with over 100,000 sales. Unfortunately, over the years a couple of problems have arisen due to the glue used on the clear, stamp-retaining strips. In the majority of cases it has dried-out, causing it to discolour and allow the strips to lift away from the black card. However, this has not affected the collectibility of the pack and it remains a popular item.

Following the initial excitement generated by the 1964 Shakespeare pack, there was a temporary decline in sales. This has led to there being fewer early packs in circulation, giving them a higher market value. The most notable is the 1964 Forth Road Bridge pack (PP4) of which only 11,450 were sold - it currently has a guide price of £375.

During the 1960s and early 1970s most commemorative stamps were available in a presentation pack, but it was not until 1976 that every stamp issue had its own pack. The Post Office viewed presentation packs as a sales tool to attract new customers and impulse buyers. They also developed the range to encourage stamp collecting in other countries, particularly Germany and Japan, by printing packs in foreign languages. In the early days, presentation packs were available to purchase in a number of public outlets, such as airports and tourist attractions. For example, the 1965 Post Office Tower pack was on sale at the Tower until decimalisation in 1971.

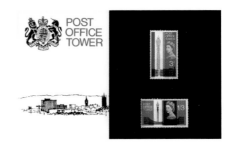

Production

In 1982, a new format was devised for the Commemorative and Definitive Packs. They became bigger and the information card opened 'up' rather than 'out'. This gave the pack designers more space to utilise and collectors noted that it made the packs easier to mount on stamp album leaves. In March 2004, there was a further change in the commemorative pack design with the majority of packs having clear, stamp-retaining strips adhered directly onto the information card, rather than the stamps being presented on a separate, black card.

Special machines were created to assist in the production of presentation packs. An early example was the Autopak, which was able to compile 2,000 presentation packs an hour. The production of Royal Mail presentation packs is now fully automated, with special equipment designed to lift and hold the stamp-retaining strip while each stamp is inserted by another machine. The stamp carrier card and the information card are then wrapped in a clear plastic sleeve to complete the process.

Printing Errors

Errors on presentation packs came about due to printer problems, such as movement in the card during printing or a colour being missed from the print. For example, the 1976 Roses Commemorative Pack (PP73) is known to be missing the pink print on the outside of the pack. Only a limited number of packs would have been affected by this so they are classified as an Error not a Type. As printing methods have developed, and more stringent product checks have been carried out, fewer examples have been observed.

Colour shifts and colour variations, whilst sometimes spectacular, have not been listed in this catalogue due to the potential varieties and quantity in circulation. However, these packs are very collectible and make interesting additions to a collection. Within the catalogue, we have noted where a pack is known to be missing a colour, on its listing.

Error Pack Values

A pack with a printed colour shift might have a value of £10 to £100, depending on how spectacular the error.

The value of a pack with a missing colour can be anything from £75 to £600, depending on how different the pack is to the original.

Promotion

Nowadays, most presentation packs are available from Post Offices and other outlets for up to a year after the stamp issue. However, some packs are only on the market for a limited period of time due to licensing restraints. For example, Royal Mail only had a licence to sell their Olympic and Paralympic issues until 31st December 2012, which meant that the Memories of London 2012 Commemorative Pack (PP450) was only available for little over three months.

Traditionally, new issues were promoted on A4-size posters affixed to walls of Post Offices around the country, but recently a special 'Wall-Window' display has been developed. The Wall-Window holds presentation packs in such a way that they are visible from both sides, thereby making them suitable for display in a window.

Royal Mail philatelic
Wall-Window display

Presentation pack categories

This catalogue has been divided into sections, each representing a different category of presentation packs.

Commemorative Packs

These are the most frequently produced and most popular packs amongst collectors. They are released by Royal Mail on the day that stamps are issued and contain an information card to provide details and images relating to the theme of the stamps.

The first Commemorative Pack was the 1964 Shakespeare Festival (PP1) which included basic information about the stamp designer and the printer. Through the years, Royal Mail has developed the significance of the information card and its role in promoting stamps and stamp collecting. However, it was not until 1976 that a Commemorative Pack was released with every stamp issue.

A number of Commemorative Packs include exclusive additional features. For example, in the 1979 Horseracing pack (PP92) there was an additional booklet containing illustrations of stamp designs by Thelwell, a famous cartoonist. The designs were not chosen for production but the Post Office wanted to include them in the pack. In later years, pack designers became more creative. The 2010 Wallace and Gromit Christmas pack had an integrated advent calendar and the 2012 Comics pack contained a mini comic strip from the first issue of the 'Dandy'.

Cartoon from a booklet of stamp designs by Thelwell. Exclusive to the 1979 Horseracing pack

Between 1987 and 1994, 13 different complimentary tickets and discount vouchers to British exhibitions and museums were included in certain Commemorative Packs. The majority have expired, however the ticket in the 1989 Lord Mayor's Show pack (PP175) is an exception and still valid today. This complimentary ticket to the Tower Bridge Exhibition has been verified and can be used against an adult admission, worth £8 in 2014.

The design of Commemorative Packs is continually evolving, with many now including a stamp miniature sheet displayed either on the front or on the reverse.

In the Commemorative and Definitive Packs sections, there are additional entries for packs produced in a foreign language, or for which a foreign language insert card was issued. These packs were first produced in the late 1960s when the Post Office was promoting British stamp collecting to the German market. From the 1968 British Paintings pack to the 1969 Investiture of The Prince of Wales pack, all were translated and printed in German, as was the 1969 Low Value Definitive Pack. However, due to disappointing sales, separate German insert cards were printed and included with the standard English pack, from the 1969 Post Office Tower pack to the 1974 Collectors Pack, when this practice ended.

Another overseas market explored by the Post Office was Japan, with insert cards produced from the 1968 British Paintings pack until the 1972 Christmas pack. The only Commemorative Pack translated into Japanese was the 1972 Royal Silver Wedding pack.

Only two packs have been issued in Welsh. The first, 1969 Investiture of The Prince of Wales, was given to the school children of Wales. The second was 1998 Diana, Princess of Wales, which has been very popular with collectors, leading to an increase in its value over recent years.

It is reported that eight insert cards were printed in Dutch, for packs from 1969 British Ships to 1971 Literary Anniversaries. It appears that only one of each was produced so they are considered likely to have been printer proofs. For this reason, we have not included them in this catalogue.

During the early years of presentation packs there was some inconsistency in production, leading to different versions, or Types, of the same pack being produced. This is particularly evident in the 1970 General Anniversaries pack (PP32) in which a catalogue of mistakes lead to the publication of eight different Types. The most well-known error is the misspelling of "Marjorie", the name of the stamp designer, as "Majorie". A lesser-known error is another spelling mistake ("decendants" instead of "descendants"), which appears in two places inside the pack. In addition to these differences, there are two versions of the Royal crest on the front of the pack, in which a chain is visible, or not visible, between the legs of the Unicorn. The rarer examples of these Types are currently valued at up to £150.

Types are sometimes evident on the Royal coat of arms, where differences are believed to have come about due to the varying print processes used during early pack production. The technique used to emboss and print the coat of arms required two dies, which may have led to the slight differences between print runs of certain packs. An example can be seen on the 1969 British Cathedrals pack (PP27).

A different Type was identified in the 1974 Famous Britons pack. Due to unexpected sales, a reprint was required but the printer used a different 'whiter' card for the second run, making the printed colours look slightly brighter than the original pack.

Definitive Packs

These packs provide information on the background to Definitive and Country stamps issued by Royal Mail. The first Definitive Packs were issued on 5th March 1969, with one pack of low value pre-decimal Machin stamps and the other with high value pre-decimal Machin stamps.

On 15th February 1971, Great Britain converted to decimal currency and the Post Office issued a new low value Definitive Pack (PPD7) on the same day. Initially, the numbering of Definitive Packs was included in the Commemoratives system but in 1983 they were split into a separate category.

Country Packs were first issued on 9th December 1970 with individual packs released for Northern Ireland, Scotland and Wales. These were originally referred to as 'Regionals' but in 1999 the Post Office relaunched them as 'Country' Packs and included England for the first time.

In 1971, after decimalisation, new issues were released for each country and, for the first time, a pack was produced for the Isle of Man. New Country Packs were produced in line with changes to postage rates or stamp design. Since 2004, single packs combining stamps from England, Scotland, Wales and Northern Ireland have been issued, rather than separate packs for each. The Country Packs for Wales are written in English and Welsh, apart from 1970 Wales (PPD5).

The only Definitive Pack to contain a booklet of stamps was 1993 Machin 1st Booklet (PPD53). This contained the first self-adhesive stamps issued by Royal Mail presented as a set of 20 1st Class stamps. Unfortunately, this first self-adhesive set has not stood the test of time and the stamps no longer peel off the backing paper.

Since 2002, Royal Mail has issued at least one Definitive Pack a year due to changes in postage rates, new values and changed colours. Also, in 2002 the design of the packs was updated with a crown and national floral emblem replacing the three lions crest used previously.

Collectors Club Packs

The Collectors Club was set up to promote stamp collecting to children and as a family activity. It became one of the largest clubs of its kind with 70,000 members worldwide. A 'new look' Collectors Club was launched in 2000 with new members receiving a collecting kit consisting of 100 used UK stamps, The Collectors Club official organiser, postcards, badge, pencil, stamp calendar and a membership card. The bi-monthly Stamp! Magazine was sent out to all members. Only three presentation packs were issued specifically for the Collectors Club and they are now difficult to obtain.

Forerunner Packs

These packs are known as Forerunners because they are considered by many to be the first presentation packs issued. They were the inspiration of Frank Langfield, who was developing the philatelic retail department of the General Post Office (GPO) by promoting stamps in the UK and the USA. They were first sold in July 1960 at the International Stamp Exhibition held at Festival Hall, London.

Four packs were created to hold the four different sets of definitive stamps available in 1960, consisting of high value Castle, low value Wildings, 'Phosphor-graphite' definitive and 'Regional' stamps. These packs were designed to hold the stamps on blue-grey card placed inside a sealed envelope with a large window to display the stamps. On the reverse of the pack were details relating to the enclosed stamps. Two versions of each pack were produced, one priced in pound sterling and the other in US dollars. The 1960 DLR Castles pack also exists without a price printed on the front. This is probably the rarest pack of all and we have only ever seen one example.

The stamps in Forerunner Packs were mounted on card but had a tendency to move around, so some collectors opened their packs to move the stamps into the correct position. Original packs were sold sealed, therefore unopened ones now have a higher market value.

Format Packs

These stamp Format Packs are specialist products issued by Royal Mail and contain gutter pairs, cylinder blocks, traffic lights or top left corner of the selvedge of certain stamp issues (i.e different formats), within a sealed cellophane cover. They were sold at face value and available from the Philatelic Bureau and selected Post Offices.

The first Format Pack we know of was for the 1998 Endangered Species stamp issue. They are now only occasionally produced; the most recent being for the 2010 Britain Alone issue, only available from the Royal Mail stand at the London 2010 International Stamp Exhibition.

(We have listed all the Format Packs we are aware of. They are not allocated 'PP' catalogue numbers as we believe that more examples might exist. Please let us know of any others for inclusion in subsequent editions of this catalogue.)

Greetings Packs

Greeting stamps were originally produced in booklet format. They were first included within a presentation pack in 1992. Each pack contains 10 1st Class stamps and a set of corresponding labels. Altogether, from 1992 to 1997, six different Greetings Packs were produced.

Inside 1994 Greetings pack

Corresponding labels

Miniature Sheet Collection Packs

Production of these Collection Packs began in 2005. Presented in durable plastic folders, they contain a complete set of the year's miniature sheets with an accompanying information card.

Inside the pack

Post & Go Packs

Post & Go Packs were introduced in 2009 and have proved popular with collectors. Originally, these packs did not carry premium pricing as they consist only of self-adhesive stamps on a simple carrier and information card. Royal Mail regularly issue these packs throughout the year, focussing on a specific theme. The theme for 2014 is British Flora.

Details of stamp content found under the stamps

Postage Due (To Pay) Packs

Four presentation packs were issued by the Post Office containing Postage Due (To Pay) labels - the first in 1971 and the last in 1994. All the packs include information on the background of 'To Pay' labels, which were introduced to Great Britain in 1914. These labels do not display the Royal portrait as they are not stamps, simply notification of the fine for incorrect postage paid at the time of sending.

Reproduction Packs

Reproduction Packs are produced to commemorate special British stamps. The first was issued in 2000 to commemorate the celebrated Penny Black. The simple pack contains a block of four Penny Black stamps printed from a new plate that was made using the original die from the Post Office archives.

Watermark effect on the back of the stamps

Significant attention to detail goes into the production of these packs, causing admiration amongst collectors. For example, the Postal Union Congress London 1929 Reproduction Pack contains stamps produced using the original die but with a watermark effect on the reverse and the word 'facsimile', to clearly distinguish them from the originals. This pack (PPR2) was issued in 2010 to tie-in with the London International Stamp Exhibition.

Smilers for Kids

The Smilers for Kids Packs were launched by the Post Office on 28th October 2008 with four designs featuring well known children's book characters; Peter Rabbit, Almond Blossom, Mr Happy and Noddy. These special packs were created to appeal to children and contain 10 self-adhesive 1st Class stamps on a sheet, plus corresponding labels. Also included in the packs were other items, such as 'new baby' announcement cards and cut-out masks for children.

Continuing the theme in 2009, another four Smilers for Kids Packs were issued, this time featuring Jeremy Fisher, Wild Cherry, Little Miss Sunshine and Big Ears.

Memorabilia inside a Smilers for Kids Pack

Year Packs

(Also known as Gift Packs and Collectors Packs)
The first Year Pack, originally called Gift Pack, was issued at the end of 1967 and contained that year's stamps. The Royal cypher, embossed in gold on the cover of the pack, made this a striking new addition to the GPO product range.

The pack includes information on the stamp printing process and details of the artists. Over 105,000 packs were sold.

1976 Year Pack designed to show contents from the back, as well as from the front

In 1968, a Gift Pack was produced containing the commemorative stamps issued between January and August that year. Strangely, the GPO also published a Collectors Pack, which contained selected stamp issues from 1967 and 1968. From 1969 to 1971, they continued to produce Collectors Packs containing selected stamps from two years, but since 1972 packs have been issued containing only one year's stamps. The only other changes since then have been the move to the current A4-size format in 1983, and the name change to Year Pack in 1994.

Year Books

Year Books were introduced by the Post Office in 1984 as a luxury item. They are hardback books contained within a rigid sleeve for protection. Each book contains an illustrated chapter on every stamp issue that year, along with a full set of the stamps for the collector to place into slip-in mounts on the appropriate pages. Since 1989, miniature sheets have also been included. In 1995, the Post Office introduced leather-bound Year Books in limited editions.

An interesting Year Book for collectors to look out for is the 1988 volume, which is the only source of an unissued 13p Christmas stamp of that year. During 1988 postage rates were increased from 13p to 14p, but the books had already been printed and the stamps enclosed. The 13p stamps had to be replaced by the new 14p stamp, but some books escaped the process. This 13p Christmas stamp is therefore extremely rare.

1988 Year Book

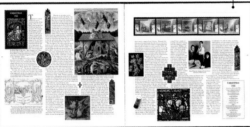

Inside the Book

Souvenir and Special Edition Packs

This section contains a wide variety of packs varying in style, content and size. They were all produced by Royal Mail and some were distributed by third parties.

The first Special Edition Pack was issued in 1969 when the British Ships Commemorative Pack was reprinted for sale on board the Cunard Line Queen Elizabeth II cruise ship. The original pack had noted that the Queen Elizabeth II "sailed on her maiden voyage to New York on 17th January 1969." However, the sailing was delayed so Cunard commissioned a reprint with corrected text reading "sails on her maiden voyage early in 1969."

To promote British stamp collecting abroad, the Post Office conducted a tour of Scandinavia in April and May 1971. For this tour, a special pack was produced (Scandinavia '71) containing the new low value decimal stamps for promotion. The pack content was translated into Danish, Swedish and Norwegian on a separate insert card.

Also in 1971, the Post Office first experimented with 'on-pack' merchandising in association with Heinz soups. Eight different Heinz soup labels had to be collected and redeemed in order to receive a special stamp pack that contained 6 x2½p Christmas stamps. The red and black pack was dispatched in a specifically designed envelope. In 1981, the Post Office and Cadbury Typhoo co-operated in promotion of a special Souvenir Pack to mark the Royal Wedding.

The Post Office introduced a new presentation pack format, the Souvenir Pack, for Belgica'72, the International Stamp Exhibition in Brussels. This pack featured the two most recent religion-themed stamp issues; 1971 Christmas and 1972 Village Churches. The illustrated booklet incorporated a slip-in mount on the inside cover for the stamps, with information on other religion-themed stamps produced by the Post Office over previous years. Later in 1972, they produced a pack to celebrate the Royal Silver Wedding; the illustrated booklet contained background information and photographs of the Royal couple. Over the years, various Souvenir Packs have been produced to mark other special events, such as the 150th Anniversary of the Penny Black.

1972 Royal Silver Wedding Souvenir Pack

Inside the Pack

In 1981, a Japanese Souvenir Pack containing the 1981 Royal Wedding stamps was produced by a British Post Office overseas agent, for the Tokyo Philatelic Show. The stamps commemorate the marriage of HRH The Prince of Wales and Lady Diana Spencer. The main text is in Japanese, with "British Post Office" in English on the reverse. When the packs were received by the Philatelic Bureau in Edinburgh, for sale to British collectors, it was discovered that the Japanese text claimed that Prince Charles had had to stand on a box for the stamp photographs to be taken. The pack was subsequently reprinted with this statement removed.

In 1986 and 1987, the Post Office experimented with the sale of special Christmas promotional packs containing a sheet of 36 x13p Christmas stamps (two panes of 18 stamps separated by a gutter). There are also examples of the 1986 pack with a barcode label added to the plastic cover, produced for selling in non-Post Office outlets.

*(Items considered outside the scope of this catalogue include
large bundle packs, generic sheet packs, hardback books,
commemorative documents and stamp/postcard packs. If demand
exists, they will be included in future editions.)*

Private Packs

Over the years, a number of individuals and organisations
have produced Private Packs featuring specific Royal Mail
stamp issues. Whilst there are many third-party Private
Packs that could be included, this catalogue lists only those
considered the most noteworthy and significant. This
selection takes into account many aspects including size,
style, content, publisher, quality, consistency and credibility.

The Post Office Missed collection (known as POM packs)
was created by Michael Morse to provide presentation
packs for the stamp issues not covered by the Post Office.
In the 1960s and 1970s, he produced 16 packs featuring
issues from the 1937 Coronation of King George VI, to the
1977 Silver Jubilee 9p issue.

Several organisations have created their own packs
to celebrate an anniversary or event. In 1972, the BBC
commemorated its 50th Anniversary by producing a special
pack as a memento for staff. The pack had text on the
outside cover only and contained three stamps that related
to the BBC.

The Dereham Stamp Centre, in Norfolk, produced a number
of Private Packs to celebrate special occasions, such as the
80th birthday of The Queen Mother and her connections
with Norfolk. This series is known as Norwich Packs.

Other Private Packs were produced to promote British
stamps abroad. For example, at the 1978 American
Philatelic Society Annual Convention in Indianapolis, a
simple pack containing that year's Horse and Cycling stamp
issues was presented.

A more recent, noteworthy, Private Pack was produced by
the National Assembly of Wales in 2006, for distribution to
its members. The pack contains a 2006 Celebrating Wales
miniature sheet and a specially designed information card
that details the history of the Assembly.

Collecting and storing packs

How to start collecting

There is a wide range of presentation packs available and whether you choose to collect a single type or more, there is something for everyone. The most recent packs can be obtained from Royal Mail at the time of each stamp issue. Older packs can be sourced at stamp shows, auctions, on eBay, and through a number of online retailers. As specialist dealers ourselves, Packs & Cards can supply the majority of the packs listed in this catalogue.

A popular way to collect is in Year Sets, where you can buy all the issues published in any one year. It can be an easy and quick way to build a collection and many dealers offer a discount if you buy this way.

2006 Year Set comprising 14 Commemorative Packs

Unfortunately, there are known to be 'fake' packs in circulation. Valuable Commemorative Packs such as 1964 Forth Road Bridge and 1998 Diana, Princess of Wales (printed in Welsh), have been forged. Tell-tale signs of a fake are the abnormal weight of the information card and pixelation in the printed images. If in doubt, ask a specialist dealer to verify the pack.

Storing presentation packs

To keep packs safe, it is advisable to store them in strong boxes or in specifically designed presentation pack albums. The most important factor is to keep them flat, in a cool, dry environment, away from direct sunlight.

The cellophane covers on early presentation packs had a tendency to shrink, causing the packs to buckle. Before placing a buckled pack in an album, it is best to remove it from the cellophane cover, to allow the pack to return to its original, flat state. Keep the original cellophane behind, or alongside, the pack.

Presentation pack album

So, there you have it in a nutshell. There has never been a better time to start or to build-upon a collection. Have fun!

Year of issue
and pack title

Stamp issue
date

1964 Shakespeare Festival (23rd April)

Marking the 400th Anniversary of the birth of William
Shakespeare, this is the first commemorative presentation
pack issued by the British Post Office. Features illustrations and
quotes from five Shakespeare plays. (Qty. sold 108,541)
Note: This pack also exists with all five stamps 'cancelled', in a
version that was given away as a promotion piece.

Quantity sold
or issued by
Royal Mail,
where known

Illustration

	Type a	Type b

PP1	1964 Shakespeare Festival		24.00	☐
	a Unicorn's collar decorated with fleur-de-lys	30.00		☐
	b Unicorn's collar in solid red	24.00		☐

Check box when
you acquire
the pack

Description of pack
types and languages

Check boxes
for specialist items

2004 Classic Locomotives (13th January)

Containing illustrations and technical specifications of six classic
steam locomotives, this pack discusses the railways they ran
on, the way they were utilised and their preservation.

Description of
pack content

CLASSIC LOCOMOTIVES
Preserving the Steam Age
Royal Mail Mint Stamps

| PP325 | 2004 Classic Locomotives (Printed no.355) | 9.00 | ☐ |

Guide price

Presentation pack
catalogue number

Number printed
on the pack

Commemorative Packs

These are the most popular packs. They are released by Royal Mail on the day that commemorative stamps are issued and contain an information card providing details and images that relate to the theme of the stamps.

Within this section, we have included packs printed in Welsh, German and Japanese, insert cards printed in a foreign language, and 'Types' where differing printing processes have led to two or more versions of the same pack.

The listed guide price for insert cards is for a card only - it does not include the relevant presentation pack.

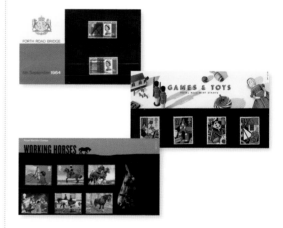

1964 Shakespeare Festival (23rd April)

Marking the 400th Anniversary of the birth of William Shakespeare, this is the first commemorative presentation pack issued by the British Post Office. Features illustrations and quotes from five Shakespeare plays. (Qty. sold 108,541)

Note: This pack also exists with all five stamps 'cancelled', in a version that was given away as a promotion piece.

	Type a	Type b

PP1	1964 Shakespeare Festival	24.00	☐
a	Unicorn's collar decorated with fleur-de-lys	30.00	☐
b	Unicorn's collar in solid red	24.00	☐

1964 Geographical Congress (1st July)

Issued to commemorate the 20th International Geographical Congress, this pack shows aspects of the changing face of Britain in 1964. (Qty. sold 29,952)

PP2	1964 Geographical Congress	140.00	☐

Also exists as an Error - Coat of arms missing

1964 Botanical Congress (5th August)

Commemorating the 10th International Botanical Congress which took place in Edinburgh. Includes illustrations and information on four plant varieties. (Qty. sold 16,140)

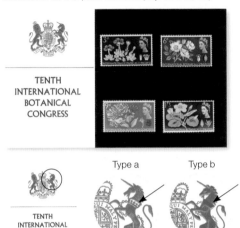

	Type a	Type b

PP3	1964 Botanical Congress	150.00	☐
a	Unicorn's collar decorated with fleur-de-lys	225.00	☐
b	Unicorn's collar in solid red	150.00	☐

1964 Forth Road Bridge (4th September)

To mark the opening, by Her Majesty The Queen, of the Forth Road Bridge, this pack contains interesting facts and figures on the construction of the bridge. (Qty. sold 11,450)

PP4	1964 Forth Road Bridge	375.00	☐

1965 Churchill (8th July)

Following his death in January 1965, this pack recounts the life of Sir Winston Churchill. (Qty. issued 38,500)

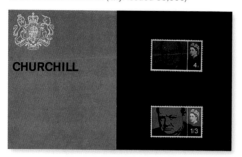

PP5   1965 Churchill   55.00 ☐
Also exists as an Error - Black text missing

1965 Anniversary of Parliament (19th July)

Commemorating the 700th Anniversary of Simon de Montfort's Parliament, this pack contains historical information on its evolution. (Qty. issued 24,450).

PP6   1965 Anniversary of Parliament   65.00 ☐

1965 Battle of Britain (13th September)

Commemorating the 25th Anniversary of the Battle of Britain, this pack recounts the German air raids on Britain between July 10th and October 31st 1940. (Qty. issued 28,524)

PP7   1965 Battle of Britain   65.00 ☐

1965 Post Office Tower (8th October)

Issued to mark the operational opening of the Post Office Tower in London in 1965, this pack contains interesting facts and figures about the Tower's capabilities. (Qty. issued 25,060)

PP8   1965 Post Office Tower   9.00 ☐

1966 Robert Burns (25th January)

Celebrating the work of Scottish poet Robert Burns (1759-1796), the pack includes four of his poems. (Qty. issued 38,968)

PP9   1966 Robert Burns   55.00 ☐

1966 Westminster Abbey (28th February)

Commemorating the 900th Anniversary of the consecration of Westminster Abbey, this pack details some of the Abbey's history. (Qty. sold 24,272)

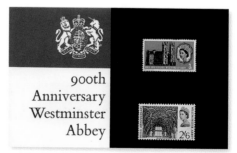

PP10   1966 Westminster Abbey   48.00 ☐

1966 Football World Cup (1st June)

Produced to commemorate the World Cup football championships of July 1966 which were hosted, and won, by England. This pack contains statistics on the four-yearly tournament. (Qty. sold 48,732) **Note:** When England won the Cup, the 4d stamp was overprinted with 'England Winners' and reissued. The Post Office did not release a seperate pack, but a Private Pack exists - see 'Post Office Missed' section.

PP11   1966 Football World Cup   17.50   ☐

1966 British Birds (15th August)

This pack discusses the most common 'British' birds and the continual interchange of birds between countries and continents during migration. (Qty. sold 42,888)

PP12   1966 British Birds   12.00   ☐

1966 British Technology (19th September)

Detailing some of the achievements in British engineering and technology over the previous 20 years, including the Hovercraft, car production, nuclear power and Jodrell Bank. (Qty. sold 35,437)

PP13   1966 British Technology   15.00   ☐

1966 Battle of Hastings (14th October)

Commemorating the 900th Anniversary of the Battle of Hastings, this pack recounts the events of William of Normandy's invasion of England and victory over Harold II, as depicted in the Bayeux Tapestry. (Qty. sold 51,332)

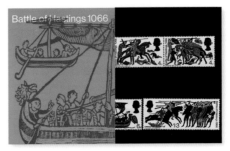

PP14   1966 Battle of Hastings   10.00   ☐

1966 Christmas (1st December)

This pack contains Britain's first adhesive Christmas stamps: they were also the first stamps designed by children in response to a national competition. Inside are eleven other designs which were commended by the judges. (Qty. sold 33,672)

PP15   1966 Christmas   12.00   ☐

1967 EFTA (20th February)

Produced to mark the achievement of free trade within the European Free Trade Association, this pack tells EFTA's history and of their goal of a single European market. (Qty. sold 42,906)

PP16   1967 EFTA   32.00   ☐

1967 British Flora (24th April)

Several British wild flowers are illustrated in this pack and many more are described as the text runs through Spring, Summer and Autumn. (Qty. sold 53,446)

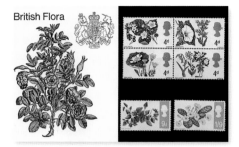

PP17   1967 British Flora   12.50   ☐
Also exists as an Error - Missing pink colour

1967 British Painters (10th July)

Celebrating the work of three British artists, L.S. Lowry, George Stubbs and Sir Thomas Lawrence, this pack gives a brief resumé of each man and a potted history of British painting. (Qty. sold 46,017)

PP18   1967 British Painters   32.00   ☐

1967 British Discovery (19th September)

Celebrating British inventions and Britain's contribution to science, this pack details the history of penicillin, television, radar and the jet engine. (Qty. sold 59,117)

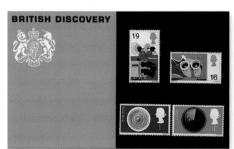

PP19   1967 British Discovery   6.00   ☐

1968 British Bridges (29th April)

Depicting man's ingenuity and daring in his battle with the elements, this pack tells of Britain's heritage of bridges spanning the ages, from Tarr Steps in Exmoor, to the M4 viaduct. (Qty. sold 69,646)

PP20   1968 British Bridges   4.00   ☐

1968 Anniversaries (29th May)

Commemorating the Anniversaries of Captain Cook's voyage of discovery, the TUC, formation of the RAF and women's Suffrage, this pack tells their stories. (Qty. sold 67, 639)

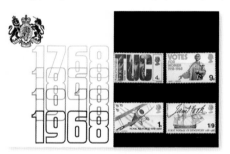

PP21   1968 Anniversaries   4.00   ☐

Also exists as an Error - Missing black text and images

1968 British Paintings (12th August)

Celebrating four famous British paintings, spanning five centuries (1575-1940), the pack also gives some information on three eminent British artists. This was the first pack to be printed in German and the first for which a Japanese insert card was produced. (Qty. sold 93,829, German Qty. sold 7,880)

PP22
front

PP22
reverse

PP22 g
reverse

PP22	1968 British Paintings	4.00	☐
g	German language pack	17.50	☐
j	Japanese insert card	200.00	☐

1968 Christmas (25th November)

This Christmas issue takes a look at the history of children's toys, with accompanying illustrations. (Qty. sold 72,474, German Qty. sold 7,298)

PP23

Type a   Type b

PP23 g

PP23	1968 Christmas		4.00	☐
a	One tuft on Unicorn's head	4.00		☐
b	Two tufts on Unicorn's head	6.00		☐
g	German language pack	17.50		☐

1969 British Ships (15th January)

This pack pays tribute to British shipbuilders and seamen, and describes six famous British ships, as illustrated on the stamps; Elizabeth Galleon, East Indiaman, SS Great Britain, Cutty Sark, RMS Mauretania, RMS Queen Elizabeth 2. (Qty. sold 116,526, German Qty. sold 4,416)

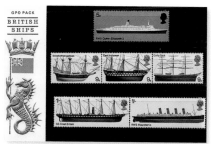

PP24

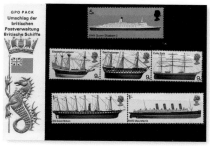

PP24 g

PP24	1969 British Ships	5.00	☐
	g German language pack	60.00	☐
	j Japanese insert card	200.00	☐

1969 Concorde (3rd March)

This pack commemorates the first flight of Concorde and tells of its origins and the collaboration between British and French Governments. (Qty. sold 100,608, German Qty. sold 2,827)

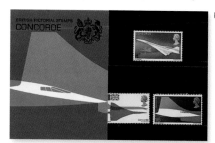

PP25

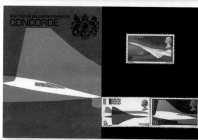

PP25 g

PP25	1969 Concorde	8.00	☐
	g German language pack	90.00	☐
	j Japanese insert card	200.00	☐

Also exists as an Error - Black text missing inside

1969 Notable Anniversaries (2nd April)

Commemorating five notable events, including details of the first non-stop flight across the Atlantic and the 1949 North Atlantic Treaty (Qty. sold 90,282, German Qty. sold 4,539)

PP26

PP26 g

PP26	1969 Notable Anniversaries	4.00	☐
	g German language pack	90.00	☐
	j Japanese insert card	200.00	☐

1969 Cathedrals (28th May)

The first of a series celebrating British Architecture, this pack describes six well-known British Cathedrals. (Qty. sold 119,828, German Qty. sold 7,200)

PP27

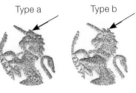

Type a   Type b

PP27 g

PP27	1969 Cathedrals (printed no.10)		5.00	☐
	a	One tuft on Unicorn's head	7.00	☐
	b	Two tufts on Unicorn's head	5.00	☐
	g	German language pack	45.00	☐
	j	Japanese insert card	150.00	☐

Also exists as an Error - Gold coat of arms missing

1969 Investiture (1st July)

Commemorating the Investiture of HRH The Prince of Wales this pack tells the history of the ceremony, dating back to 1284 when the first Prince of Wales was presented to the people of Caernarvon by King Edward I. (Qty. sold 256,709; German Qty. sold 9,360; Welsh Qty. sold 146,958)

PP28

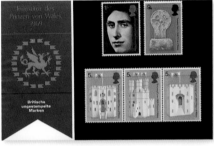

PP28 g

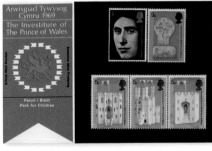

PP28 w

The Investiture of The Prince of Wales
プリンス・オブ・ウエールズの叙位

PP28	1969 Investiture		2.50	☐
	g	German language pack	45.00	☐
	j	Japanese insert card	50.00	☐
	w	Welsh language pack given to school children in Wales	17.50	☐

1969 Post Office Technology (1st October)

This pack discusses some of the Post Office's technical achievements and was the first one also available with a German insert card. (Qty. sold 104,230)

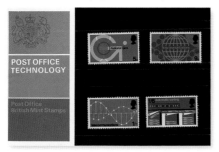

PP29	1969 Post Office Technology		3.00	☐
g	German insert card [PL(P)2041]	7.50		☐
j	Japanese insert card	7.50		☐

1969 Christmas (26th November)

This pack features illustrations of medieval artistic interpretations of the Nativity, in a variety of mediums. (Qty. sold 121,454)
Note: this is the first pack to have a printed reference number. Interestingly, it is number '14' - see Introduction for information.

PP30	1969 Christmas (printed no.14)		4.00	☐
g	German insert card [PL(P)2050]	9.00		☐
j	Japanese insert card [PL(P)2049]	9.00		☐

1970 British Rural Architecture (11th February)

This pack explains the relationship between geology, architecture and early methods of construction in Scotland, England, Wales and Northern Ireland. (Qty. sold 116,983)

Type a   Type b

PP31	1970 Rural Architecture (printed no.15)		4.50	☐
a	One tuft on Unicorn's head	4.50		☐
b	Two tufts on Unicorn's head	9.00		☐
g	German insert card [PL(P)2057A]	10.00		☐
j	Japanese insert card [PL(P)2057B]	10.00		☐

1970 General Anniversaries (1st April)

Celebrating five British Anniversaries, this pack features the Declaration of Arbroath (1320), birth of Florence Nightingale (1820), International Co-operative Alliance (1895), Voyage of the Mayflower (1620), and the Royal Astronomical Society (1820). (Qty. sold 120,564)

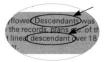
'Chain' missing

'Chain' visible

Marjorie Saynor
The 1s and 1s 9d stamp designed by Marjorie S. underwent her preli...

'Marjorie' correct

Majorie Saynor
The 1s and 1s 9d stamp designed by Marjorie S. underwent her prel...

'Majorie' incorrect
Back of pack

...flower Descendants was the records, plans etc. of t...lined descendant over 18...

'Descendants' correct

...flower Decendants was the records, plans etc. of t...lined decendant over 18...

'Decendants' incorrect
Inside pack

ALLGEMEINE JAHRESTAGE	THE STAMPS 切手		

PP32	1970 General Anniversaries (printed no.16)	4.00	☐
a	Chain missing. Marjorie correct Descendants correct	4.00	☐
b	Chain missing. Marjorie correct Descendants incorrect	150.00	☐
c	Chain missing. Marjorie incorrect Descendants correct	150.00	☐
d	Chain missing. Marjorie incorrect Descendants incorrect	8.50	☐
e	Chain visible. Marjorie correct Descendants correct	4.00	☐
f	Chain visible. Marjorie correct Descendants incorrect	150.00	☐
h	Chain visible. Marjorie incorrect Descendants correct	150.00	☐
i	Chain visible. Marjorie incorrect Descendants incorrect	8.50	☐
g	German insert card [PL(P)2073A]	10.00	☐
j	Japanese insert card [PL(P)2073B]	10.00	☐

1970 Literary Anniversaries (3rd June)

Marking the centenary of the death of Dickens and the bicentenary of the birth of Wordsworth, this pack contains information about the lives of both men. (Qty. sold 113,770)

LITERARISCHE GEDENKTAGE DICKENS UND WORDSWORTH	THE STAMPS 切手

PP33	1970 Literary Anniversaries (printed no.17)	5.00	☐
g	German insert card [PL(P)2082A]	10.00	☐
j	Japanese insert card [PL(P)2082B]	10.00	☐

1970 British Commonwealth Games (15th July)

Issued on the eve of the ninth British Commonwealth Games, this pack contains photos and facts about the purpose-built facilities. (Qty. sold 114,209)

PP34	1970 British Commonwealth Games (printed no.19)		4.00	☐
g	German insert card [PL(P)2093A]	9.00		☐
j	Japanese insert card [PL(P)2093B]	9.00		☐

1970 Philympia (18th September)

Issued for the International Stamp Exhibition held at Olympia, London, this pack gives information about the exhibition and its three main sponsors; the RPS, the BPA and the PTS. (Qty. sold 110,916)

PP35	1970 Philympia (printed no.21)		4.00	☐
g	German insert card [PL(P)2104A]	9.00		☐
j	Japanese insert card [PL(P)2104B]	9.00		☐

1970 Christmas (25th November)

This pack contains illustrations and information about the De Lisle Psalter, from which the stamp designs were derived. (Qty. sold 138,632)

PP36	1970 Christmas (printed no.22)		4.00	☐
g	German insert card [PL(P)2112A]	9.00		☐
j	Japanese insert card [PL(P)2112B]	9.00		☐

Also exists as an Error - Black text missing inside

1971 Ulster '71 Paintings (16th June)

Ulster '71 was a major festival and exhibition, held to promote Northern Ireland. This pack contains information about the impressive scale of the exhibition and the artists whose paintings are reproduced on the stamps. (Qty. sold 100,257)

1971 Literary Anniversaries (28th July)

Commemorating the 150th Anniversary of the death of John Keats, Bicentenary of the death of Thomas Gray and Bicentenary of the birth of Sir Walter Scott, with details of each man. This pack was issued with a spelling mistake, so some contained an Erratum note. (Qty. sold 104,724)

Type a   Type b

PP38	1971 Literary Anniversaries (printed no.32)	7.00	☐
	g German insert card [PL(P)2158A]	9.00	☐
	j Japanese insert card [PL(P)2158B]	9.00	☐

Also exists as an Error - Black text missing

PP37	1971 Ulster '71 Paintings (printed no.26A)	7.00	☐
	a Missing chain under Unicorn's legs	7.00	☐
	b Chain visible under Unicorn's legs	13.50	☐
	g German insert card [PL(P)2151A]	9.00	☐

1971 General Anniversaries (25th August)

Marking anniversaries of The British Legion, City of York and The Rugby Football Union, this pack gives a brief history, and images, of each. (Qty. sold 94,059)

PP39	1971 General Anniversaries (printed no.32A)	7.00	☐
	g German insert card [PL(P)2166A]	9.00	☐
	j Japanese insert card [PL(P)2166B]	9.00	☐

1971 Universities (22nd September)

This continuation of the British Architecture series is devoted to that of some of our modern university buildings with details of the four buildings featured on the enclosed stamps. (Qty. sold 87,159)

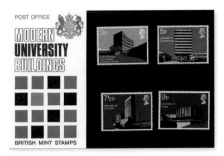

Type a   Type b

PP40	1971 Universities (printed no.33)		9.00	☐
	a One tuft on Unicorn's head	9.00		☐
	b Two tufts on Unicorn's head	9.00		☐
	g German insert card [PL(P)2174A]	10.00		☐
	j Japanese insert card [PL(P)2174B]	10.00		☐

1971 Christmas (13th October)

This pack contains illustrations and information about the stained glass windows of Canterbury Cathedral. (Qty. sold 113,276)

PP41	1971 Christmas (printed no.35)	6.00	□
	g German insert card [PL(P)2182A]	8.00	□
	j Japanese insert card [PL(P)2182B]	8.00	□

Also exists as an Error - Gold coat of arms missing

1972 British Polar Explorers (16th February)

The lives and discoveries of four of Britain's most intrepid explorers are celebrated in this pack. (Qty. sold 103,676)

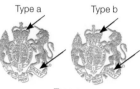

Type a   Type b

Type c

PP42	1972 British Polar Explorers (printed no.39)	7.00	□
	a Solid crown, flower missing between Unicorn's legs	7.00	□
	b Solid crown, flower visible between Unicorn's legs	8.50	□
	c Decorative crown, flower visible between Unicorn's legs	17.00	□
	g German insert card [PL(P)2197A]	9.00	□
	j Japanese insert card [PL(P)2197B]	9.00	□

Also exists as an Error - Gold coat of arms missing

1972 General Anniversaries (26th April)

Marking anniversaries of Ralph Vaughan Williams, Tutankhamun and HM Coastguard, this pack gives a brief history and images of each. (Qty. sold 89,113)

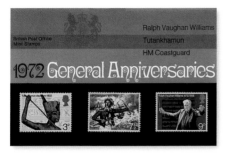

PP43	1972 General Anniversaries (printed no.40)	7.00	☐
g	German insert card [PL(P)2204A]	8.00	☐
j	Japanese insert card [PL(P)2204B]	8.00	☐

1972 Village Churches (21st June)

Another issue in the British Architecture series. In this pack, various parts of ancient churches, from early Saxon to late Perpendicular, are illustrated and explained. (Qty. sold 109,512)

PP44	1972 Village Churches (printed no.41)	9.00	☐
g	German insert card [PL(P)2211A]	10.00	☐
j	Japanese insert card [PL(P)2211B]	10.00	☐

1972 BBC & Broadcasting History (13th September)

Commemorating the 50th Anniversary of the BBC and 75th Anniversary of Marconi/Kemp experiments, this pack includes information about the history of the BBC and Marconi's invention of broadcasting. (Qty. sold 99,453) **Note:** The BBC produced their own version of this pack - see 'Private Packs' section.

Type a   Type b

PP45	1972 BBC & Broadcasting History (printed no.43)	5.00	☐
a	Gold letters on a white background	5.00	☐
b	White letters on a gold background	20.00	☐
g	German insert card [PL(P)2224A]	7.50	☐
j	Japanese insert card [PL(P)2224B]	7.50	☐

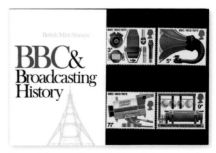

Also exists as an Error - Gold coat of arms missing

1972 Christmas (18th October)

This pack details the subject matter and design of the enclosed stamps, and describes the artist's creative process. (Qty. sold 105,740)

PP46 | 1972 Christmas (printed no.44) | | 4.00 | □
| g | German insert card [PL(P)2233A] | 7.50 | □
| j | Japanese insert card [PL(P)2233B] | 7.50 | □

1972 Silver Wedding (20th November)

Celebrating the 25th Wedding Anniversary of The Queen, this pack recalls previous issues associated with the Royal family. (Qty. sold 140,050; Japanese Qty. issued 8,500)

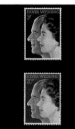

PP45

PP45 j

PP47 | 1972 Silver Wedding (printed no.45) | | 3.00 | □
| g | German insert card [PL(P)2243A] | 7.00 | □
| j | Japanese language pack | 6.00 | □

1973 European Communities (3rd January)

This pack marks 1st January 1973 as the day that the United Kingdom became a member of the European Communities, along with Ireland, Denmark and the six existing members. (Qty. sold 105,850)

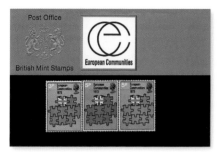

| PP48 | 1973 European Communities (printed no.48) | 2.50 | □ |
| | g German insert card [PL(P)2259A] | 7.00 | □ |

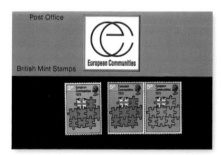

Also exists as an Error - Gold coat of arms missing

1973 Oak Tree (28th February)

Highlighting a Government-sponsored campaign to encourage the planting of trees and focussing on the Oak, this pack illustrates this great British tree and discusses its many uses through history. (Qty. sold 96,722)

| PP49 | 1973 Oak Tree (printed no.49) | 2.50 | □ |
| | g German insert card [PL(P)2267] | 7.00 | □ |

1973 British Explorers (18th April)

Celebrating five British explorers; Sir Francis Drake, Sir Walter Raleigh, Charles Stuart, David Livingstone and Sir Henry Morton Stanley, this pack details their lives and explorations. (Qty. sold 102,950).

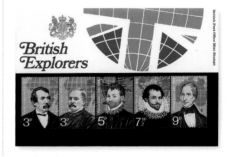

| PP50 | 1973 British Explorers (printed no.50) | 4.00 | □ |
| | g German insert card [PL(P)2275] | 7.00 | □ |

1973 County Cricket (16th May)

In 1873 a series of meetings took place to draw up official rules for cricket. This pack tells the story and marks the Centenary of County Cricket. (Qty. sold 97,870)

| PP51 | 1973 County Cricket (printed no.51) | 4.50 | □ |
| | g German insert card [PL(P)2283] | 7.50 | □ |

1973 British Painters (4th July)

Celebrating the work of two British painters, Sir Joshua Reynolds and Sir Henry Raeburn, this pack gives a synopsis of the life and work of each man. (Qty. sold 104,830)

| PP52 | 1973 British Painters (printed no.52) | 3.00 | □ |
| | g German insert card [PL(P)2291] | 7.50 | □ |

1973 Inigo Jones (15th August)

Marking the 400th Anniversary of the birth of Inigo Jones, celebrated architect and designer, this pack gives a factual account of his work along with several illustrations. (Qty. sold 99,320)

| PP53 | 1973 Inigo Jones (printed no.53) | 3.00 | □ |
| | g German Insert Card [PL(P)2302] | 7.50 | □ |

1973 Parliamentary Conference (12th September)

Commemorating the 19th Commonwealth Parliamentary Conference, which was held in Britain for the first time since 1961. Contains information about the CPA and an annotated illustration of the Palace of Westminster. (Qty. sold 86,010)

| PP54 | 1973 Parliamentary Conference (printed no.54) 3.00 | □ |
| | g German insert card [PL(P)2311] | 7.00 | □ |

1973 Royal Wedding (14th November)

Produced to commemorate the marriage of HRH Princess Anne to Captain Mark Phillips, this pack contains photos of the couple and gives brief details of their lives. (Qty. sold 130,390)

Type a   Type b

Type c   Type d

PP55	1973 Royal Wedding (printed no.56)	2.50	☐
	a No flower between Unicorn's legs.		
	Dog cut off edge of picture	4.75	☐
	b No flower between Unicorn's legs.		
	Whole dog in picture	2.50	☐
	c Flower between Unicorn's legs.		
	Dog cut off edge of picture	4.75	☐
	d Flower between Unicorn's legs.		
	Whole dog in picture	2.50	☐
	g German insert card [PL(P)2320]	7.00	☐

1973 Christmas (28th November)

This pack tells the story behind the song 'Good King Wenceslas' and discusses the custom of singing Christmas carols. (Qty. sold 107,070)

Type a   Type b

PP56	1973 Christmas (printed no.57)	2.50	☐
	a Narrow red band 4mm	3.75	☐
	b Thick red band 6mm	2.50	☐
	g German insert card [PL(P)2327]	7.00	☐

1974 The Horse Chestnut (27th February)

This pack continues the theme of British trees, with illustrations and information about the Horse Chestnut. (Qty. sold 93,680)

| PP57 | 1974 The Horse Chestnut (printed no.58) | 2.00 | ☐ |
| g | German insert card [PL(P)2337] | 7.00 | ☐ |

1974 Fire Service (24th April)

Marking the Bicentenary of The Fire Prevention (Metropolis) Act of 1774, this illustrated pack tells the history of the Fire Service and how local fire brigades came to be. (Qty. sold 118,010)

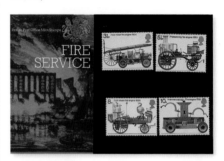

	Type a	Type b

PP58	1974 Fire Service (printed no.60)		3.50	☐
a	No flower between Unicorn's legs	3.50		☐
b	Flower between Unicorn's legs	7.00		☐
g	German insert card [PL(P)2352]	8.00		☐

Also exists as an Error - Gold coat of arms missing

1974 UPU (12th June)

The Universal Postal Union was founded on 9th October 1874 and this pack, marking its centenary, tells of how it came about and its main role. (Qty. sold 105,550)

Type a   Type b

PP59	1974 UPU (printed no.64)	3.50	☐
a	No flower between Unicorn's legs	3.50	☐
b	Flower between Unicorn's legs	5.00	☐
g	German insert card [PL(P)2360]	8.00	☐

Also exists as an Error - Gold coat of arms missing

1974 Great Britons (10th July)

This pack honours four of Britain's great medieval warriors; Robert the Bruce, Owain Glyndwr, The Black Prince, Henry V, with a synopsis and illustration of each in battledress. (Qty. sold 130,600)

PP60
Type a

PP60
Type b

PP60 g

PP60	1974 Great Britons (printed no.65)	3.50	☐
a	Printed on cream card	3.50	☐
b	Reprint on white card	9.00	☐
g	German insert card [PL(P)2368]	7.00	☐

1974 Churchill Centenary (9th October)

Celebrating the Centenary of the birth of Winston Churchill, this pack covers his career from 1899 to 1942. (Qty. sold 146,050)

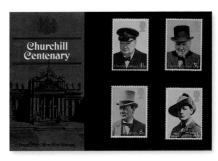

PP61	1974 Churchill Centenary (printed no.66)	3.50	☐
g	German insert card [PL(P)2379]	7.00	☐

1974 Christmas (27th November)

This pack gives a brief history of church roof bosses and details those featured on the enclosed stamps, which depict scenes from the Christmas story. (Qty. sold 129,020)

PP62	1974 Christmas (printed no.67)	3.00	☐
g	German insert card [PL(P)2390]	7.00	☐

1975 Turner (19th February)

Continuing the British Painters series, this issue celebrates the Bicentenary of the birth of JMW Turner and tells his story alongside images of two pen and ink studies. (Qty. sold 122,020)

PP63	1975 Turner (printed no.69)	2.50	☐

1975 European Architectural Heritage Year
(23rd April)

European Architectural Heritage Year marked the end of a campaign to protect buildings and areas of architectural interest. This pack gives a brief history of the five buildings featured on the enclosed stamps. (Qty. sold 114,140)

PP64	1975 European Architectural Heritage Year (printed no.70)	2.50	☐

1975 Sailing (11th June)

Commemorating the Bicentenary of the Royal Thames Yacht Club and the Centenary of the Royal Yachting Association, this pack discusses the celebratory events planned for the year. Contains photos of various types of sailing craft. (Qty. sold 125,610)

PP65	1975 Sailing (printed no.71)	2.00	☐

1975 Railways (13th August)

This pack celebrates the 150th Anniversary of the first public steam railway by recounting the history of Stephenson's Locomotion and evolution of the modern High Speed Train. Contain photos of locomotives through the years. (Qty. sold 134,700)

| PP66 | 1975 Railways (printed no.72) | 3.50 | ☐ |

1975 Parliament (3rd September)

The Inter-Parliamentary Union was founded in 1889 by an Englishman, William Cremer, and a Frenchman, Frederick Passey. This pack tells their story and marks the occasion of the 62nd Conference. (Qty. sold 113,770)

| PP67 | 1975 Parliament (printed no.74) | 1.50 | ☐ |

Also exists as two Errors - Purple missing on cover
Purple missing inside

1975 Jane Austen (22nd October)

To commemorate the Bicentenary of the birth of Jane Austen, this pack tells her story. Apart from Royalty, she was only the second woman to be commemorated on British stamps. (Qty. sold 129,400)

| PP68 | 1975 Jane Austen (printed no.75) | 5.00 | ☐ |

Also exists as an Error - Black text missing on reverse

1975 Christmas (26th November)

This Christmas pack looks at the significance of angels and their celestial hierarchy. Contains several poems about various types of angels. (Qty. sold 124,970)

| PP69 | 1975 Christmas (printed no.76) | 3.00 | ☐ |

1976 The Telephone (10th March)

Commemorating the Centenary of the first telephone call, made by Alexander Graham Bell on 10th March 1876, this pack tells of the development of national phone lines to connect the whole country. (Qty. sold 136,430)

| PP70 | 1976 The Telephone (printed no.78) | 2.50 | ☐ |

1976 Social Reformers (28th April)

A tribute to the pioneers of social reform in the 19th century, this illustrated pack details the life-changing work of Thomas Hepburn, Robert Owen, Lord Shaftesbury and Elizabeth Fry. (Qty. sold 117,880)

| PP71 | 1976 Social Reformers (printed no.79) | 2.50 | ☐ |

1976 Bicentennial of American Independence (2nd June)

This pack contains the history behind the American Declaration of Independence, with accompanying illustrations. (Qty. sold 140,650)

| PP72 | 1976 Bicentennial of American Independence (printed no.80) | 1.50 | ☐ |

1976 Roses (30th June)

This pack marks the Centenary of the Royal National Rose Society with information about some celebratory events and details of the hybrid tea rose, shrub rose, sweet briar and floribunda illustrated on the enclosed stamps. (Qty. sold 138,010)

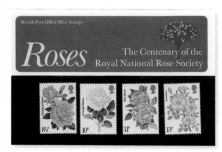

| PP73 | 1976 Roses (printed no.81) | 2.50 | ☐ |

Also exists as an Error - Pink missing on cover and reverse

1976 British Cultural Traditions (4th August)

Written in English and Welsh, this pack celebrates the 800th Anniversary of the Royal National Eisteddfod and discusses early cultural traditions across Britain.

| PP74 | 1976 British Cultural Traditions (printed no.82) | 2.50 | ☐ |

1976 William Caxton (20th September)

Illustrated with wood-cut engravings, this pack pays tribute to William Caxton by recounting his introduction of printing into England in 1476.

PP75   1976 William Caxton (printed no.83)   2.50   ☐

1976 Christmas (24th November)

Celebrating renowned English medieval embroidery, this pack details the Christmas scenes featured on the enclosed stamps, which are taken from a collection at the Victoria and Albert Museum. (Qty. sold 138,985)

PP76   1976 Christmas (printed no.87)   2.50   ☐

Also exists as an Error - Black text missing

1977 Racket Sports (12th January)

This pack describes the evolution of four of the most popular and widespread sports; tennis, table tennis, badminton and squash. With illustrations and photos throughout. (Qty. sold 142,943)

PP77   1977 Racket Sports (printed no.89)   2.50   ☐

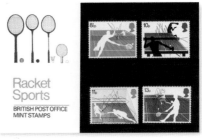

Also exists as an Error - Red image missing

1977 Chemistry (2nd March)

Commemorating the Centenary of the Royal Institute of Chemistry, this pack discusses some of the ways that chemists have reshaped society. (Qty. sold 144,499)

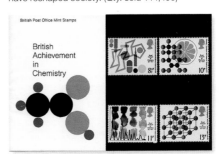

PP78   1977 Chemistry (printed no.92)   2.50   ☐

Also exists as an Error - Blue text missing inside pack

1977 Silver Jubilee (11th May)

Marking the 25th Anniversary of The Queen's accession to the throne, this pack contains a brief history of her family life from 1952 to 1977. (Qty. sold 476,017)

PP79   1977 Silver Jubilee (printed no.94)   2.00   ☐

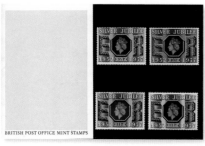

Also exists as an Error - Silver text missing on cover

1977 Heads of Government (8th June)

Commemorating the 1977 summit conference in London of the Commonwealth Heads of Government, this pack details its role and includes a map of the member countries. (Qty. sold 162,582)

PP80   1977 Heads of Government (printed no.95) 1.50   ☐

1977 British Wildlife (5th October)

Some of Britain's best loved wild animals are detailed and illustrated in this pack, which was designed to make children and adults more aware of the nation's wildlife heritage. (Qty. sold 227,696)

PP81   1977 British Wildlife (printed no.96)   2.00   ☐

1977 Christmas (23rd November)

Celebrating 'The Twelve Days of Christmas', this pack tells of the song's origins and its popularity as a parlour game. Illustrated with the twelve 'gifts'. (Qty. sold 206,225)

PP82   1977 Christmas (printed no.97)   2.00   ☐

1978 Energy (25th January)

In the year during which North Sea oil and natural gases came ashore in large quantities for the first time, this pack discusses the demand for fuel and the uncertainty of future energy supplies. (Qty. sold 139,500)

PP83   1978 Energy (printed no.99)   2.00   ☐

1978 Historic Buildings (1st March)

Continuing the British Architecture series, this pack is devoted to Royal Palaces and Castles, and details those featured on the enclosed stamps. With accompanying illustrations. (Qty. sold 159,450)

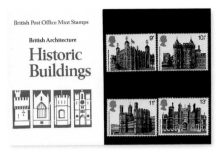

PP84 1978 Historic Buildings (printed no.100)   2.00   □

1978 25th Anniversary of Coronation (31st May)

Commemorating the 25th Anniversary of The Queen's Coronation, this pack is full of photos and information about the regalia used during the ceremony in 1953. (Qty. sold 279,060)

PP85 1978 25th Anniversary of Coronation
(printed no.101)   2.00   □

1978 Horses (5th July)

Marking the Centenary of the Shire Horse Society of England, this pack looks at the lineage of all thoroughbreds, the work of Shire horses and popularity of Welsh ponies and Shetland's. Contains a photo of each breed.
(Qty. sold 182,360)

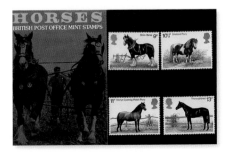

PP86 1978 Horses (printed no.102)   1.75   □

1978 Cycling (2nd August)

In 1878, the world's first national cycling competitions took place and this pack marks their Centenary by telling the history of cycle design. (Qty. sold 176,670)

PP87 1978 Cycling (printed no.103)   1.75   □

1978 Christmas (22nd November)

This pack focusses on the tradition of singing Christmas carols. With accompanying illustrations. (Qty. sold 219,630)

PP88 1978 Christmas (printed no.104)   1.75   □

1979 Dogs (7th February)

Continuing the 'Animal' theme that commenced with the 1977 Wildlife pack, this pack discusses the four breeds featured on the enclosed stamps, with a photo of each. (Qty. sold 231,300)

PP89 1979 Dogs (printed no.106)   2.00   □

1979 British Flowers (21st March)

Four of the best-loved wild flowers in Britain are described and illustrated in this pack, along with details of their preferred habitats. (Qty. sold 250,690)

PP90 1979 British Flowers (printed no.107)   1.75   □

1979 Direct Elections (9th May)

In advance of the first Direct Elections to the European Assembly on 7-10 June 1979, this pack explains how they came to be. (Qty. sold 252,990)

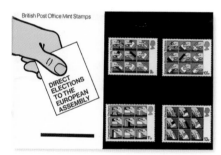

PP91 1979 Direct Elections (printed no.108)   1.75   □

1979 Horseracing (6th June)

Commemorating the 200th running of the Derby, this pack discusses horseracing of all types and contains images from several races. (Qty. sold 326,810). Note: These packs included an additional booklet of stamp designs by Thelwell, the famous cartoonist.

PP92 1979 Horseracing (printed no.109)   1.75   □

1979 Year of the Child (11th July)

This pack celebrates the famous books of four great British authors - Lewis Carroll, Beatrix Potter, Kenneth Grahame and A.A. Milne - with brief details of each, plus accompanying illustrations. (Qty. sold 374,010)

PP93   1979 Year of the Child (printed no.110)   1.75   □

1979 Rowland Hill (22nd August)

Marking the the Centenary of the death of Sir Rowland Hill (1795-1879) this pack tells the story of his life and Postal Reform. Contains photos and images of early posters, a Penny Black and other related memorabilia. (Qty. sold 370,510)

PP94   1979 Rowland Hill (printed no.111)   2.50   □

1979 Police (26th September)

Containing the history of the Metropolitan Police Act of 1829, introduced by Sir Robert Peel, Home Secretary, this pack also includes illustrations and images of early policing, plus modern day photos. (Qty. sold 347,810)

PP95   1979 Police (printed no.112)   1.60   □

1979 Christmas (21st November)

This pack looks back beyond the familiar festive story to the Norse Festival of Yule and, later, the rituals of the Roman festival Saturnalia. Also contains passages from the Bible. (Qty. sold 400,310)

PP96   1979 Christmas (printed no.113)   1.75   ☐

Also exists as an Error - Pink missing on cover

1980 British Birds (16th January)

Detailing four popular British waterbirds and their habitats, this pack marks the Centenary of the Wild Bird Protection Act of 1880. Contains an illustration of each breed.

PP97   1980 British Birds (printed no.115)   2.00   ☐

1980 Liverpool and Manchester Railway
(12th March)

The world's first regular passenger-carrying railway is celebrated in this pack, which details some of its history alongside attractive images of paintings produced during construction.

PP98   1980 Liverpool and Manchester Railway
(printed no.116)   1.60   ☐

1980 'London 1980' (9th April)

In advance of the International Stamp Exhibition at Earls Court, this pack was produced to promote the show. It mentions some of the exhibits and illustrates the Post Office stand design.

PP99   1980 'London 1980' (printed no.117)   1.60   ☐

1980 London Landmarks (7th May)

This pack contains historic details of the iconic London landmarks that are featured on the enclosed stamps, particularly of their original use and/or design.

PP100   1980 London Landmarks (printed no.118)   1.60   ☐

1980 Famous People (9th July)

Four female Victorian writers are honoured in this pack with a synopsis of each woman's life and work.

PP101   1980 Famous People (printed no.119)   1.60   ☐

Also exists as an Error - Red text missing

1980 British Conductors (10th September)

Celebrating Britain's musical heritage, this pack details four of the nation's most distinguished conductors - Sir Henry Wood, Sir Thomas Beecham, Sir Malcolm Sargent and Sir John Barbirolli. Contains a photo of each man and illustrations of three famous concert halls.

PP102   1980 British Conductors (printed no.120)   1.60   ☐

1980 Sport (10th October)

Four British Sporting Centenaries are marked in this pack with the history of each: Amateur Athletics Association, Welsh Rugby Union, formation of the Amateur Boxing Association and the first Test match against Australia.

PP103   1980 Sport (printed no.121)   1.60   ☐

1980 Christmas (19th November)

This pack tells of the tradition of Christmas decorations in the home, particularly that of bringing in a tree and mistletoe.

PP104   1980 Christmas (printed no.122)   1.60   ☐

1981 Folklore (6th February)

This pack details the history of the four traditional customs that are featured on the enclosed stamps and contains illustrations to represent each one.

PP105   1981 Folklore (printed no.124)   1.50   ☐

1981 International Year of Disabled People
(25th March)

The UN General Assembly chose 1981 as International Year of Disabled People and this pack discusses various types of disability. Contains illustrations by Elizabeth Twistington Higgins MBE.

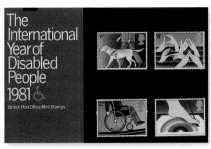

PP106   1981 International Year of Disabled People
(printed no.125)   1.50   ☐

1981 Butterflies (13th May)
The preferred habitats and life cyles of four butterflies are featured in this pack, with accompanying illustrations.

PP107   1981 Butterflies (printed no.126)   2.00   ☐

1981 The National Trusts (24th June)
Commemorating the Golden Jubilee of the National Trust for Scotland, this pack details the four 'properties' featured on the enclosed stamps, along with an illustration of each.

PP108   1981 The National Trusts (printed no.127)   2.00   ☐

1981 Royal Wedding (22nd July)
In anticipation of the marriage of The Prince of Wales and Lady Diana Spencer, this pack gives details of Charles's peerage and their close family links through Diana's father, Earl Spencer. Contains several photos of the happy couple.

PP109   1981 Royal Wedding (printed no.127A)   3.00   ☐

1981 Duke of Edinburgh's Award (12th August)
Celebrating the 25th Anniversary of the Scheme, this pack tells the story behind the Duke of Edinburgh's Award and details the four sections it comprises. Contains photos of candidates participating in the Scheme.

PP110   1981 Duke of Edinburgh's Award
(printed no.128)   1.75   ☐

1981 Fishing (23rd September)
Organisations in the fishing industry designated 1981 as Fishermen's Year and this pack discusses the important contribution of Britain's fishermen to the national economy.

PP111   1981 Fishing (printed no.129)   1.75   ☐

1981 Christmas (18th November)

The theme of this pack is 'Through the eyes of a child' and it contains details of the young designers of the enclosed stamps, who were Blue Peter competition winners.

PP112   1981 Christmas (printed no.130)   1.75   ☐

1982 Charles Darwin (10th February)

Commemorating the Centenary of the death of Charles Darwin, this pack focusses on three native species of the Galapagos Islands. Contains 14 images relating to Darwin's life and work.

PP113   1982 Charles Darwin (printed no.131)   1.75   ☐

1982 Youth Organisations (24th March)

This pack commemorates the contribution made by youth organisations to British society and culture. Contains photos of the founders of the Boy's Brigade, Scouts and YMCA.

PP114   1982 Youth Organisations (printed no.133) 1.75   ☐

1982 British Theatre (28th April)

The CEPT theme for 1982 was Historical Events and this pack takes a look at the history of British theatre, from Burbage's purpose-built playhouse in 1576 to the opening of the Barbican Centre.

PP115   1982 British Theatre (printed no.134)   1.75   ☐

1982 Maritime Heritage (16th June)

In tribute to Britain's naval and maritime tradition, this pack details three distinguished figures of the Admiralty and their flagships, plus Henry VIII and the Mary Rose. Contains various naval images and photos.

PP116   1982 Maritime Heritage (printed no.136)   2.50   ☐

1982 British Textiles (23rd July)

Celebrating the 250th Anniversary of the birth of Sir Richard Arkwright, this pack discusses some of the most well-known textile designers and the history of decorating fabrics. Contains images of early printing machines.

PP117   1982 British Textiles (printed no.137)   2.50   ☐

1982 Information Technology (8th September)

Supported by government and industry, 1982 was designated Information Technology Year. This pack discusses the advances and use of IT in everyday life, plus Royal Mail's technology designed to handle bulk mailing.

PP118   1982 Information Technology
         (printed no.138)   2.00   ☐

1982 British Motor Cars (13th October)

To highlight and promote British Industry, this pack features modern cars and their famous vintage counterparts. Produced to coincide with the staging of the British Motor show, held at the NEC, Birmingham.

PP119   1982 British Motor Cars (printed no.139)   2.50   ☐

Also exists as an Error - Silver missing

1982 Christmas Carols (17th November)

The Christmas Carols featured on the enclosed stamps are individually illustrated in this pack alongside the first verse and the origin of each one.

PP120   1982 Christmas Carols (printed no.140)   2.50   ☐

1983 British River Fishes (26th January)

The four river fish featured on the enclosed stamps are illustrated in this pack along with details of their habitats and feeding habits.

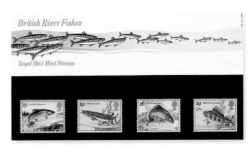

PP121   1983 British River Fishes (printed no.142)   2.00   ☐

1983 Commonwealth Day (9th March)

To commemorate Commonwealth Day on 14th March 1983, this pack discusses the spirit and goals of the Commonwealth and contains photos of The Queen visiting various countries.

PP122   1983 Commonwealth Day (printed no.143)   2.00   ☐

1983 Engineering Achievements (25th May)

This pack features three notable British engineering achievements; the Humber Bridge, Thames Flood Barrier and oilfield emergency support vessel Iolair, with facts, figures and photos of each.

| PP123 | 1983 Engineering Achievements (printed no.144) | 1.75 | ☐ |

1983 The British Army (6th July)

The British Army is recognised as one of the world's most efficient. This pack gives a synopsis of five well-known regiments and images of their badges.

| PP124 | 1983 The British Army (printed no.145) | 2.00 | ☐ |

1983 British Gardens (24th August)

This pack discusses changes in garden design and use of plants from the 17th to 20th century. Includes illustrations of flowers and images of famous landscape gardeners.

| PP125 | 1983 British Gardens (printed no.146) | 2.00 | ☐ |

1983 British Fairs (5th October)

The earliest record of a fair in Britain dates from Roman times. This pack details the history of fairs and their original purpose of trading, and includes illustrations of early carousels and entertainers.

| PP126 | 1983 British Fairs (printed no.147) | 2.00 | ☐ |

1983 Christmas (16th November)

The spirit of Christmas is represented in this pack by various verses from the Bible, the Koran, and several poems, which can all be related to the images on the enclosed stamps.

| PP127 | 1983 Christmas (printed no.148) | 2.50 | ☐ |

1984 Heraldry (17th January)

Commemorating 500 years of the College of Arms, this pack explains the use of 'arms' and their study, known as heraldry. Contains images of pages from medieval Rolls of Arms.

| PP128 | 1984 Heraldry (printed no.150) | 2.50 | ☐ |

1984 Cattle (6th March)

This pack commemorates the Centenary of the Highland Cattle Society and the Bicentenary of the Royal Highland and Agricultural Society of Scotland, with descriptions of the five breeds featured on the enclosed stamps.

PP129   1984 Cattle (printed no.151)   2.00   ☐

1984 Urban Renewal (10th April)

This pack marks the 150th Anniversaries of the Royal Institute of British Architects and the Chartered Institute of Building, and describes the process of urban renewal in four British cities.

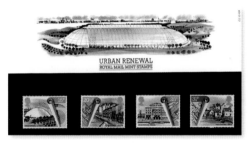

PP130   1984 Urban Renewal (printed no.152)   2.00   ☐

1984 Europa (15th May)

Commemorating the 25th Anniversary of the Conference of European Posts and Telecommunications Administrations and the holding of the second direct elections to the European Parliament, this pack details the background of each.

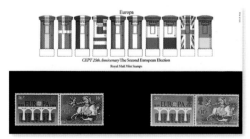

PP131   1984 Europa (printed no.153)   2.00   ☐

1984 Greenwich (26th June)

Commemorating the Centenary of worldwide adoption of the Greenwich meridian, this pack explains the need for, and importance of, a single system of time and longitude. Includes a photo of the Royal Observatory and an earthshot from Apollo II.

PP132   1984 Greenwich (printed no.154)   2.00   ☐

1984 The Royal Mail (31st July)

Marking the Bicentenary of the first mail coach run from Bristol and Bath to London in 1784, this pack traces the development of the service alongside photos of a Mail Coach guard's typical equipment.

PP133   1984 The Royal Mail (printed no.155)   2.50   ☐

1984 The British Council (25th September)

Commemorating the 50th Anniversary of the British Council, this pack lists its aims and how they are achieved, with accompanying images.

PP134   1984 The British Council (printed no.156)   2.00   ☐

1984 Christmas (20th November)

This Christmas pack discusses the link between Christian beliefs and artistic styles through the centuries, with particular focus on the themes of the enclosed stamps. Contains images of paintings, stained glass and frescoes depicting the nativity.

PP135   1984 Christmas (printed no.157)   2.00   □

1985 Famous Trains (22nd January)

A tribute to five of Britain's famous titled trains, this pack is full of facts and figures about each one. It also marks the 150th Anniversary of the founding of the Great Western Railway (GWR).

PP136   1985 Famous Trains (printed no.159)   4.00   □

1985 Insects (12th March)

This pack describes the habits and habitats of the five insects featured on the enclosed stamps. With accompanying photos.

PP137   1985 Insects (printed no.160)   3.00   □

1985 British Composers (14th May)

In European Music Year, this pack coincided with the 300th Anniversary of the birth of George Frideric Handel. It celebrates the lives and works of Handel, Holst, Delius and Elgar.

PP138   1985 British Composers (printed no.161)   3.00   □

1985 Safety at Sea (18th June)

This pack was issued following the 11th Conference of the International Association of Lighthouse Authorities and contains facts and figures about the search and rescue services called-on by HM Coastguard.

PP139   1985 Safety at Sea (printed no.162)   3.00   □

1985 Royal Mail (30th July)

Marking the 350th Anniversary of the proclamation, by Charles I, that the Royal Mail could be used by the public, this pack discusses and illustrates how postal services have developed since the late 19th century.

PP140   1985 Royal Mail (printed no.163)   3.00   □

1985 Arthurian Legend (3rd September)

Celebrating Sir Thomas Malory's epic work 'Le Morte D'Arthur', edited and printed by William Caxton in 1485, this fully illustrated pack discusses the possible sources of his stories.

PP141   1985 Arthurian Legend (printed no.164)   3.00   ☐

1985 British Films (8th October)

To celebrate British Film Year, this pack looks back at a handful of the many great names which earned British film its reputation. Contains stills from some of the most well-known productions.

PP142   1985 British Films (printed no.165)   3.00   ☐

1985 Christmas (19th November)

The origins of Pantomime date back to Roman times. This pack tells how it developed through the centuries to become the popular Christmas-time show enjoyed today. Contains illustrations and images of old advertising posters.

PP143   1985 Christmas (printed no.166)   3.00   ☐

1986 Industry Year (14th January)

The Industry Year was initiated by the RSA to promote the importance of industry in Britain. This pack details the three main aims of the scheme with accompanying illustrations throughout.

PP144   1986 Industry Year (printed no.168A)   3.00   ☐

1986 Halley's Comet (18th February)

Halley's Comet returns to the vicinity of the Sun about every 76 years and 1986 was one of those occasions. This pack provides facts and figures about the comet along with illustrations and an image of pages from Halley's notebook.

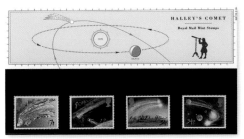

PP145   1986 Halley's Comet (printed no.168B)   3.00   ☐

1986 60th Birthday of Her Majesty (21st April)

Celebrating The Queen's 60th birthday, this pack gives some insight into her life through the decades. Contains accompanying photos throughout.

PP146   1986 60th Birthday of Her Majesty
        (printed no.170)   4.00   ☐

1986 Nature Conservation (20th May)

Highlighting the importance of conservation, this pack features information and photos of the four species represented on the enclosed stamps and their natural habitats.

PP147   1986 Nature Conservation (printed no.171)   3.00   ☐

1986 Medieval Life (17th June)

This pack is a study of how the Domesday Book was compiled and of some of its content. Contains a photo of Great Domesday and various images relating to medieval life.

PP148   1986 Medieval Life (printed no.172)   3.00   ☐

1986 Sport (15th July)

In the year of the 13th Commonwealth Games, this pack discusses the dedication and training required to be a top-flight athlete and includes photos from various sporting events.

PP149   1986 Sport (printed no.173)   3.00   ☐

1986 The Royal Wedding (22nd July)

Marking the marriage of HRH Prince Andrew to Sarah Ferguson, this pack gives a synopsis of each one's education and career up to the time of their engagement. Includes various photos.

PP150   1986 The Royal Wedding (printed no.174)   2.50   ☐

1986 Royal Air Force (16th September)

This pack tells of the outstanding achievements of Sir Hugh Trenchard, the commanders who succeeded him and the aircraft they operated. Contains archive photos of flying squadrons and their planes.

PP151   1986 Royal Air Force (printed no.175)   4.00   ☐

1986 Christmas (18th November)

The theme for this pack is Christmas Customs and it details five traditional customs that still survive, or exist in historical accounts. With accompanying illustrations.

PP152   1986 Christmas (printed no.176)   3.00   ☐

1987 Flowers (20th January)

Celebrating the work of photographer Alfred Lammer, this pack details the four flowers featured on the enclosed stamps and shows images of them in their natural habitats.

PP153   1987 Flowers (printed no.178)   3.00   ☐

1987 Sir Isaac Newton (24th March)

Commemorating the 300th Anniversary of the publication of Newton's 'Principia', this pack tells the story of the genius who effectively established modern science. Contains illustrations of his theories in practice.

PP154   1987 Sir Isaac Newton (printed no.179)   3.00   ☐

1987 British Architects in Europe (12th May)

Four British architects each have an example of their work featured in this pack with accompanying information about the structural design. There is also a very brief resumè of each man.

PP155   1987 British Architects in Europe
(printed no.180)   3.00   ☐

1987 St John Ambulance (16th June)

To commemorate the Centenary of the St John Ambulance Brigade, this pack tells of its origins, the invaluable aid given through both World Wars and continuing humanitarian work. Illustrated throughout. **Note:** Some of these packs included an organ Donor Card.

PP156   1987 St John Ambulance (printed no.181)   3.00   ☐

1987 Scottish Heraldry (21st July)

In the 300th Anniversary year of the revival of the Most Ancient and Most Noble Order of the Thistle, this pack details the associated heraldry featured on the enclosed stamps. Contains illustrations of the Badges and photos inside the Thistle Chapel.

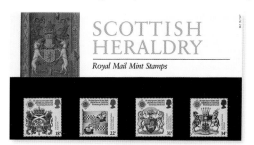

PP157   1987 Scottish Heraldry (printed no.182)   3.00   ☐

1987 Victorian Britain (8th September)

100 years after Queen Victoria's Golden Jubilee, this pack recalls some of the great achievements of the Victorian Age, along with accompanying images and illustrations.

PP158   1987 Victorian Britain (printed no.183)   3.00   ☐

1987 Studio Pottery (13th October)

Commemorating the Centenary of the birth of Bernard Leach, this pack discusses the history of British studio pottery and its development in the hands of several other influential potters. Contains photos of some modern pots, artists and their tools.

PP159   1987 Studio Pottery (printed no.184)   3.00   ☐

1987 Christmas (17th November)

This pack simply contains a magical Christmas story for children, presented to look like a book. There is also a photo of some festive fare.

PP160   1987 Christmas (printed no.185)   3.00   ☐

1988 The Linnean Society (19th January)

Celebrating the world's oldest learned body devoted to biology and natural history, this pack tells of the origin of the Linnean Society and its ongoing work. Contains images of biological books. **Note:** Some of these packs included a free ticket to the Natural History Museum, when bought with an adult ticket.

PP161   1988 The Linnean Society (printed no.187)   3.00   ☐

1988 The Welsh Bible (1st March)

Written in English and Welsh this pack marks the publication in 1988 of the New Welsh Bible, with details of its origins in 1567 and subsequent revisions up to 1588. Contains images of the Title page of several Bible editions.

PP162   1988 The Welsh Bible (printed no.188)   3.00   ☐

1988 Sport (22nd March)

In the year of the Olympic Games in Seoul, this illustrated pack celebrates four British sporting associations by looking at the popularity of gymnastics, skiing, lawn tennis and football.

PP163   1988 Sport (printed no.189)   3.00   ☐

1988 Transport and Communications (10th May)

Transport and Communication was the CEPT theme for 1988 and this pack looks back at some of the transport and mail services of 1938. Contains details of the 'Queen Elizabeth' and the 'Mallard', plus photos of modern modes of transport.

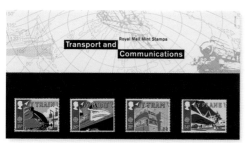

PP164   1988 Transport and Communications (printed no.190)   3.00   ☐

1988 Australian Bicentenary (21st June)

Written by author Thomas Keneally, this pack gives his personal view of Australia, shaped around the images on the enclosed stamps. Contains illustrations of Captain Cook and early settlement, plus photos of the modern-day landscape.

PP165   1988 Australian Bicentenary (printed no.191)   3.00   ☐

1988 Armada (19th July)

Marking the fourth Centenary of the defeat of the Spanish Armada, this pack tells of the cause of the conflict and opens to reveal a map showing how the battle was fought. Also contains images of salvaged artifacts and other illustrations. **Note:** Some of these packs included a free ticket to the Armada Exhibition at National Maritime Museum, Greenwich.

PP166   1988 Armada (printed no.192)   3.00   ☐

1988 Edward Lear (6th September)

A prolific artist and writer, Edward Lear's life is celebrated in this pack which discusses his fine ornithological draughtsmanship, alongside the famous Nonsense books and songs. Contains many examples of his illustrations, watercolours and sketches.

PP167   1988 Edward Lear (printed no.193)   3.00   ☐

1988 Christmas (15th November)

This pack opens to reveal images of Christmas cards and gives a brief background as to how this traditional exchange of greetings developed.

PP168   1988 Christmas (printed no.194)   3.00   ☐

1989 Birds (17th January)

Commemorating the Centenary of the RSPB, this pack details how they carry out their work and some of the problems they face. Inside is an image of a water-colour by a young ornithologist, Bridget Edwards. **Note:** Some of these packs included a free ticket to RSPB Reserves, valid for three months.

PP169   1989 Birds (printed no.196)   4.00   ☐

1989 Food and Farming (7th March)

Celebrating British Food and Farming Year, this pack looks at food production by region and shows a UK map of farming methods. Contains images of food and agriculture. **Note:** Some of these packs included a free ticket to the VIP Preview Day at ASDA Festival of Food and Farming, Hyde Park, London.

PP170   1989 Food and Farming (printed no.197)   3.00   ☐

1989 Anniversaries (11th April)

This pack commemorates the four events that are featured on the enclosed stamps, giving a brief history of each. **Note:** Some of these packs included a free set of postcards.

PP171   1989 Anniversaries (printed no.198)   3.00   ☐

1989 Games & Toys (16th May)

Featuring photos of old games and toys throughout, this pack tells how some of the best-loved childhood favourites were developed.

PP172   1989 Games & Toys (printed no.199)   4.00   ☐

1989 Industrial Archaeology (4th July)

To celebrate Museums Year, this pack tells the stories of four industrial sites of historical significance, as featured on the enclosed stamps. Contains photos, images and illustrations pertaining to each site.

PP173   1989 Industrial Archaeology
(printed no.200)   3.00   ☐

1989 Microscopes (5th September)

Commemorating 150 years of the Royal Microscopical Society, this pack delves into microscopy from Hooke's 'Micrographia' in 1665, to IVF in the 20th century. Contains various microscopic images.

PP174   1989 Microscopes (printed no.201)   3.00   ☐

1989 The Lord Mayor's Show (17th October)

This pack celebrates the tradition of the Lord Mayor's Show with details of the procession route, mention of Dick Whittington's election, and images of some of the Lord Mayor's regalia.
Note: Some of these packs included a free ticket to Tower Bridge Exhibition, Museum and Walkways. The ticket has no expiry date and is therefore still valid.

PP175	1989 The Lord Mayor's Show (printed no.202)	4.00	☐

1989 Christmas (14th November)

800 years after completion, Ely Cathdral is the feature of this pack, which details its history and the commitment over 100 years to build it. Contains photos of the interior and some of the stained glass windows.

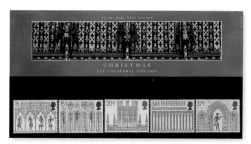

PP176	1989 Christmas (printed no.203)	3.00	☐

1990 RSPCA (23rd January)

This pack commemorates the 150th Anniversary of the RSPCA's Royal Charter and discusses the vital role of the Society in the protection, rescue and care of animals. Contains photos of various aspects of the Society's work.

PP177	1990 RSPCA (printed no.205)	4.50	☐

1990 Europa (6th March)

Written by journalist and novelist Cliff Hanley, this pack gives his thoughts on his home town of Glasgow. Contains photos of the buildings featured on the enclosed stamps.

PP178	1990 Europa (printed no.206)	3.00	☐

1990 The Queen's Awards (10th April)

Celebrating the 25th Anniversary of The Queen's Awards Scheme, this pack gives the application criteria and mentions some previous winners.

PP179	1990 The Queen's Awards (printed no.207)	3.00	☐

1990 Kew Gardens (5th June)

Commemorating the 150th Anniversary of Kew Gardens as a national institution, this pack points out the importance of plant and tree conservation. Contains photos from the Gardens and several images of botanical artist Marianne North's work.

PP180   1990 Kew Gardens (printed no.208)   3.00   ☐

1990 Thomas Hardy (10th July)

To commemorate the 150th Anniversary of the birth of Thomas Hardy, this pack celebrates his work and gives a synopsis of his life. Contains a map of 'South Wessex', Hardy's name for Dorset, showing his pseudonyms for real places.

PP181   1990 Thomas Hardy (printed no.209)   3.00   ☐

1990 HM The Queen Mother (2nd August)

This pack celebrates the 90th birthday of the Queen Mother by looking at her life and remarkable capacity to adapt to whatever role was demanded of her. Contains archive and private photos.

PP182   1990 HM The Queen Mother
(printed no.210)   5.00   ☐

1990 Gallantry (11th September)

Marking the 50th Anniversary of the George Cross, this pack explains the meaning of the five Crosses and Medals featured on the enclosed stamps.

PP183   1990 Gallantry (printed no.211)   3.00   ☐

1990 Astronomy (16th October)

Written by Patrick Moore, the focus of this pack is the telescopes that revolutionised the outlook of astronomy, from Herschel's telescope to Jodrell Bank. With accompanying photos and illustrations.

PP184   1990 Astronomy (printed no.212)   3.00   ☐

1990 Christmas (13th November)

Fully illustrated throughout, this pack contains a Christmas story written by author Susan Hill CBE.

PP185   1990 Christmas (printed no.213)   3.00   ☐

1991 Dogs (8th January)

Celebrating the Bicentenary of the Royal Veterinary College, plus centenaries of Cruft's and the National Canine Defence League, this pack gives the history behind each organisation and features some of George Stubbs' paintings of dogs.

PP186   1991 Dogs (printed no.215)   4.00 ☐

1991 Scientific Achievements (5th March)

This pack discusses the scientific achievements of Whittle, Watt, Faraday and Babbage; the latter two of whom also aided Rowland Hill's invention of the Penny Post. **Note:** Some of these packs included a child's free ticket to the Science Museum, London.

PP187   1991 Scientific Achievements (printed no.216) 3.00 ☐

1991 Europe in Space (23rd April)

Europe in Space was CEPT's chosen theme for 1991 and this pack features several of the most important European observatories and astronomical discoveries.

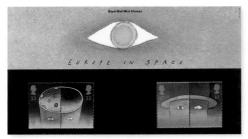

PP188   1991 Europe in Space (printed no.217)   4.00 ☐

1991 Sport (11th June)

Designated a Year of Sport, in 1991 Britain played host to the World Student Games and the finals of the Rugby World Cup. This pack discusses some of the history of both events.

PP189   1991 Sport (printed no.218)   3.00 ☐

1991 Roses (16th July)

This prettily illustrated pack pays tribute to one of the most popular species of flowers and details the varieties shown on the enclosed stamps. **Note:** Some of these packs included a free ticket to the Gardens of the Rose, St Albans.

PP190   1991 Roses (printed no.219)   5.00 ☐

1991 Dinosaurs (20th August)

Full of information about early scientific knowledge of dinosaurs, this pack focusses on the work of Richard Owen who coined the word 'dinosaur' in 1841. **Note:** Some of these packs included a child's free ticket to the Natural History Museum, London.

PP191   1991 Dinosaurs (printed no.220)   5.00 ☐

1991 Maps (17th September)

Commemorating the Bicentenary of the founding of Ordnance Survey, this illustrated pack tells the organisation's story, beginning with General William Roy in 1746. **Note:** Some of these packs included a free ticket to Autumn Stampex.

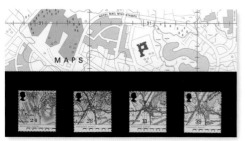

PP192   1991 Maps (printed no.221)   3.00   ☐

1991 Christmas (12th November)

To celebrate Christmas 1991, this pack tells of the lavishly illustrated 14th century manuscript known as Acts of Mary and Jesus, and details the decorated illuminations used on the enclosed stamps.

PP193   1991 Christmas (printed no.222)   3.00   ☐

1992 Wintertime (14th January)

Celebrating the most forbidding but often most beautiful of the seasons, this pack discusses the animals featured on the enclosed stamps; Fallow Deer, Brown Hare, Fox, Redwing and Welsh Mountain Sheep.

PP194   1992 Wintertime (printed no.224)   3.00   ☐

1992 Happy & Glorious (6th February)

Commemorating the anniversary of The Queen's Accession on 6th February 1952, this pack includes her own words on some of the issues she faced during the first 40 years of her reign.

PP195   1992 Happy & Glorious (printed no.225)   3.00   ☐

1992 Tennyson (10th March)

To mark the Centenary of the death of Alfred, Lord Tennyson, this pack gives the story of his life from being first published in 1826, to his final work 'Crossing the Bar' in 1889.

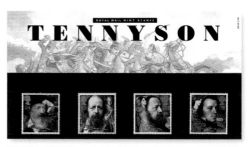

PP196   1992 Tennyson (printed no.226)   3.00   ☐

1992 Europa (7th April)

This pack celebrates the 500th Anniversary of Christopher Columbus's voyage to the New World, which was the theme of the CEPT of 1992. It also includes some information on the impending Olympic and Paralympic Games, and Expo '92.

PP197   1992 Europa (printed no.227)   3.00   ☐

1992 The Civil War (16th June)

Marking the 350th Anniversary of the beginning of the English Civil War, including the famous Battle of Naseby fought on 14th June 1645. The pack contains various interesting extracts plus a facsimile of the death warrant of Charles I.

PP198   1992 The Civil War (printed no.228)   3.00   ☐

1992 Gilbert & Sullivan (21st July)

Celebrating the 150th Anniversary of the birth of Arthur Sullivan, this pack features comic operas such as The Pirates of Penzance and The Mikado, which he and William Gilbert wrote together in the late 1800s.

PP199   1992 Gilbert & Sullivan (printed no.229)   3.00   ☐

1992 The Green Issue (15th September)

The Green Issue was the result of a children's competition and this pack shows their ideas for stamps about the environment, expressed in words as well as pictures.

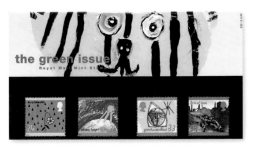

PP200   1992 The Green Issue (printed no.230)   3.00   ☐

1992 Single European Market (13th October)

In advance of the Single European Market coming into effect on 1st January 1993, this pack contains a reminder of how, and why, it came into being.

PP201   1992 Single European Market
         (printed no.231)   2.00   ☐

1992 Christmas (10th November)

Celebrating the transcendental beauty of stained glass windows in our churches and cathedrals, this pack focusses on the work of artists of the Arts and Crafts Movement and features pictures of their designs.

PP202   1992 Christmas (printed no.232)   3.50   ☐

1993 Swans (19th January)

There has been a swannery at Abbotsbury since a Benedictine Abbey was founded there in Anglo-Saxon times. The pack discusses the hazards that swans face and the swanherd's job to protect them. **Note:** Some of these packs included a free ticket to Abbotsbury Swannery.

PP203   1993 Swans (printed no.234)   5.00   ☐

1993 Marine Timekeepers (16th February)

Commemorating the 300th Anniversary of the birth of John Harrison, inventor of the chronometer, this pack tells his story and features pictures of his first four marine timekeepers, H1 to H4. **Note:** Some of these packs included £1.50 off a Passport ticket to all sites at Historic Maritime Greenwich.

PP204   1993 Marine Timekeepers (printed no.235)   3.00   ☐

1993 Orchids (16th March)

Issued on the occasion of the 14th World Orchid Conference, this pack contains illustrations and photos of four popular specimens selected from the approximated 25,000 known species.

PP205   1993 Orchids (printed no.236)   4.00   ☐

1993 Art in the 20th Century (11th May)

Art in the 20th Century was the theme adopted by Europe's postal administrations in 1993. As Royal Mail's contribution, this pack features the work of four of Britain's modern artists; Henry Moore, Edward Bawden, Stanley Spencer and Ben Nicholson.

PP206   1993 Art in the 20th Century
(printed no.237)   3.00   ☐

1993 Roman Britain (15th June)

This pack tells of the Roman conquest of Britain, beginning in AD43, the opposition to it in Wales and Scotland, and the 'Romanisation' that remains evident today.

PP207   1993 Roman Britain (printed no.238)   3.00   ☐

1993 Inland Waterways (20th July)

Marking the 200th Anniversary of the authorisation for the Grand Junction Canal, this pack is full of photos and information about the era of 'Canal Mania' and life on the inland waterways of Britain.

PP208   1993 Inland Waterways (printed no.239)   3.00   ☐

1993 Autumn (14th September)

Celebrating the beauty of Autumn, this illustrated pack marks the season of Halloween, The Lord Mayor's Show and the St. Leger horse race.

PP209   1993 Autumn (printed no.240)   3.00   ☐

1993 Sherlock Holmes (12th October)

In tribute to the renowned author Sir Arthur Conan Doyle, this pack tells his story from the first appearance of Sherlock Holmes and Dr Watson in 1887, to Doyle's final book 'The Case Book of Sherlock Holmes', published in 1927.

PP210   1993 Sherlock Holmes (printed no.241)   5.50   ☐

1993 Christmas (9th November)

Full of illustrations by Quentin Blake, this pack commemorates the 150th Anniversary of the publication of Charles Dickens' 'A Christmas Carol' and gives an insight into a Dickensian Christmas.

PP211   1993 Christmas (printed no.242)   3.00   ☐

1994 The Age of Steam (18th January)

The first age of steam in Britain lasted for 143 years and changed society on a scale never before experienced. This pack celebrates the locomotives that embodied the railway in all its works. **Note:** Some of these packs included a child's free ticket to the National Railway Museum, York.

PP212   1994 The Age of Steam (printed no.244)   5.00   ☐

1994 25th Anniversary of Investiture (1st March)

Commemorating the 25th Anniversary of the Investiture of HRH The Prince of Wales, this pack focusses on his love of painting and gives his thoughts on using watercolour.

PP213   1993 25th Anniversary of Investiture
(printed no.245)   3.00   ☐

1994 Pictorial Postcards (12th April)

Celebrating classic comic postcards which, by the 1930s, appeared in every seaside town in the UK. **Note:** Some of these packs included £5 off a family ticket into Blackpool Tower.

PP214   1994 Pictorial Postcards (printed no.246)   3.00   ☐

1994 Channel Tunnel (3rd May)

This pack tells the fascinating story of the construction of the Channel Tunnel, from approval of the winning scheme to 'breakthrough' in 1990, and beyond.

PP215   1994 Channel Tunnel (printed no.247)   3.00   ☐

1994 D-Day (6th June)

Commemorating the day, during World War II, that the great invasion of Europe began. This pack and the enclosed stamps are an evocation and record of events of those heroic days.

PP216   1994 D-Day (printed no.248)   3.00   ☐

1994 Golf (5th July)

To celebrate the 250th Anniversary of the Honourable Company of Edinburgh Golfers, this pack features four well-known holes at Muirfield, Carnoustie, Royal Troon and Turnberry.

PP217   1994 Golf (printed no.249)   3.00   ☐

1994 Summertime (2nd August)

This pack highlights the quintessential British events of Cowes Week, cricket at Lord's, Wimbledon, the Royal Welsh Show and the Highland Games, complete with photos from each.

PP218   1994 Summertime (printed no.250)   3.00   ☐

1994 Medical Discoveries (27th September)

This pack takes a look at the technological advances that have transformed medical diagnostics, including MRI, CT scans and Ultrasound imaging, and the pioneers who developed them.

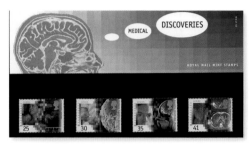

PP219   1994 Medical Discoveries (printed no.251)   3.00   ☐

1994 Christmas (1st November)

In the International Year of the Family, this Christmas pack celebrates The Nativity by opening-out to feature Dolci's painting 'Adoration of the Magi'. The pack is also cleverly designed to be used as an advent calendar.

Inside the pack is an advent calendar

PP220   1994 Christmas (printed no.252)   3.00   ☐

1995 Cats (17th January)

Exploring the special relationship between cats and humans, this pack contains the story of their domestication since the Ancient Egyptians first brought them in from the cold.

	Type a	Type b

PP221	1995 Cats (printed no.254)		4.50	☐
a	No 'smoke' from the chimney	4.50		☐
b	'Smoke' rising from the chimney	16.00		☐

1995 Springtime (14th March)

In this pack, internationally-renowned sculptor Andy Goldsworthy, whose work features on the stamps, discusses his working methods.

PP222	1995 Springtime (printed no.255)	3.00	☐

1995 The National Trust (11th April)

Celebrating 100 years of The National Trust, this pack tells of the three founders and some of the very many properties, gardens and countryside that the Trust preserves and protects.

PP223	1995 The National Trust (printed no.256)	3.00	☐

1995 Peace and Freedom (2nd May)

To mark the 125th Anniversary of the British Red Cross and the 50th Anniversary of the United Nations, this pack details the principles and importance of both organisations.

PP224	1995 Peace and Freedom (printed no.257)	3.00	☐

1995 Science Fiction (6th June)

Celebrating the works of HG Wells, this pack marks the Centenary of the publication of The Time Machine, one of the most influential of his science fiction titles, and gives a reminder of his other great stories.

PP225	1995 Science Fiction (printed no.258)	4.00	☐

1995 Shakespeare's Globe (8th August)

This illustrated pack gives the history of The Globe theatre, from the early days of 1595, under the partnership of Burbage and Shakespeare, to its short relocation and modern re-creation by Wanamaker and Crosby.

PP226   1995 Shakespeare's Globe (printed no.259) 4.00   ☐

1995 Communications (5th September)

To commemorate the 200th Anniversary of Rowland Hill's birth and the Centenary of Marconi's first effective transmissions, this pack honours their significant contribution to modern communications by outlining their inventions.

PP227   1995 Communications (printed no.260)   3.00   ☐

1995 Rugby League Centenary (3rd October)

Marking the Centenary of the birth of Rugby League, this pack features an evocative poem by Steve Ellis and some atmospheric black and white photography.

PP228   1995 Rugby League Centenary
(printed no.261)   3.00   ☐

1995 Christmas Robins (30th October)

Full of colourful illustrations, this pack is all about one of Britain's favourite birds, and features an imaginary letter from Robin Redbreast to Jenny Wren.

PP229   1995 Christmas Robins (printed no.262)   4.00   ☐

1996 Robert Burns (25th January)

Commemorating the Bicentenary of Burns' death, this pack focusses on the tradition of a Burns Supper, from the opening recital of Selkirk Grace to singing Auld Lang Syne at its close.

PP230   1996 Robert Burns (printed no.264)   3.00   ☐

1996 Wildfowl & Wetlands Trust (12th March)

To commemorate the 50th Anniversary of the WWT, this pack tells how Peter Scott's vision for a wildfowl research organisation at Slimbridge became a reality and is now a world-renowned authority in conservation.

PP231   1996 Wildfowl & Wetlands Trust
(printed no.265)   3.00   ☐

1996 Centenary of Cinema (16th April)

Since the first picture show at the Empire, Leicester Square, film-goers have been drawn to the magic of the silver screen. This pack takes an affectionate look at going to 'the pictures' and lists some Oscar-winning British films.

PP232   1996 Centenary of Cinema (printed no.266) 3.00   ☐

1996 Football Legends (14th May)

Inside this pack, Jimmy Greaves gives his thoughts on the modern game, the impending Euro96 Championship and the five legendary players who are honoured on the stamps.

PP233   1996 Football Legends (printed no.267)   3.00   ☐

1996 Olympics & Paralympics (9th July)

In anticipation of the 1996 Games, this pack contains an A to Z of Olympic and Paralympic facts and figures.

PP234   1996 Olympics & Paralympics
(printed no.268)   4.00   ☐

1996 Women of Achievement (9th July)

Celebrating the achievements of five British women who were each pioneers in their fields, this pack gives a brief glimpse into the lives of Dorothy Hodgkin, Margot Fonteyn, Elisabeth Frink, Daphne du Maurier and Marea Hartman.

PP235   1996 Women of Achievement
(printed no.269)   3.00   ☐

1996 Children's TV Characters (3rd September)

The first children's TV series was broadcast in 1946 and was the beginning of some enduring relationships between puppets and presenters. This pack opens out into a photo of some early favourites and features pop-ups of Spotty Dog and Dangermouse.

PP236   1996 Children's TV Characters
(printed no.270)   4.00   ☐

1996 Classic Sports Cars (1st October)

Featuring five loved and admired British sports cars, this pack includes an illustration and brief history of each, plus engine capacity, performance and price when new.

PP237   1996 Classic Sports Cars (printed no.271) 5.00   ☐

1996 Christmas (28th October)

This highly-stylised pack contains an analysis of the Nativity story, in the opinion of the writer, and describes the illustrations on the enclosed stamps.

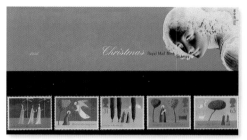

PP238   1996 Christmas (printed no.272)   5.00   ☐

1997 Henry VIII. The Great Tudor (21st January)

450 years after his death, this extended-length pack tells the dramatic story of the reign of Henry VIII and the great ministers and wives who fell victim to him. Along with the stamp showing Henry, there are also six stamps depicting his wives.

PP239   1997 Henry VIII. The Great Tudor
(printed no.274)   8.50   ☐

1997 Missions of Faith (11th March)

This pack marks 1,400 years since the Italian bishop Augustine landed on the Kent coast at the end of his pilgrimage from Rome, and gives details of three pilgrimages to follow in his footsteps in 1997.

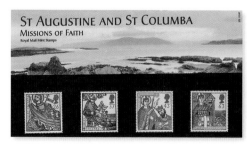

PP240   1997 Missions of Faith (printed no.275)   3.00   ☐

1997 Tales of Terror (13th May)

Featuring four horror stories of the 19th century that remain amongst the most significant of all time, this pack discusses the creation of Dracula, Frankenstein, Jekyll & Hyde and the Hound of the Baskervilles. Contains illustrations and stills from movie posters and Hammer Films Productions.

PP241   1997 Tales of Terror (printed no.276)   4.00   ☐

1997 Architects of the Air (10th June)

Written by Sir Norman Foster, this pack gives a brief history of the work of five engineering designers who transformed aviation by creating the Lancaster Bomber, Spitfire, Mosquito, Meteor and Hurricane.

PP242   1997 Architects of the Air (printed no.277)   4.00   ☐

1997 All The Queen's Horses (8th July)

Her Majesty The Queen is an acknowledged expert owner and breeder of horses. This pack honours two of her carriage horses from The Mews and two mounts from the Household Cavalry by describing them, their breeding, and their duties.

PP243   1997 All The Queen's Horses
(printed no.278)   4.00   ☐

1997 Post Offices (12th August)

Marking the Centenary of Britain's most southerly mainland post office, The Lizard in Cornwall, this pack tells the story of three successive generations of the Tiddy family who ran it from 1897 to 1988. It remains a post office to date.

PP244   1997 Post Offices (printed no.279)   3.00   ☐

1997 Enid Blyton (9th September)

Commemorating 100 years since her birth, this unusual pack opens to reveal an integrated, illustrated booklet, and gives a reminder of the prolific Enid Blyton's most well-known stories.

Inside the pack is an integrated booklet

PP245   1997 Enid Blyton (printed no.280)   3.50   ☐

1997 Christmas Crackers (27th October)

Celebrating the tradition of Christmas crackers, this pack tells the story of their invention by Tom Smith in the 1840s. Contains pictures of typical cracker contents along with some puzzles that are answered on the back of the pack.

PP246   1997 Christmas Crackers (printed no.282)   4.00   ☐

1997 Royal Golden Wedding (13th November)

To commemorate the 50th Anniversary of the Royal marriage, this elegant pack contains several facts about the spectacular wedding day, along with one of the official photos. Note: This pack is printed with an issue date of 7th October. It's release was delayed to 13th November as a mark of respect, following the death of Princess Diana.

PP247   1997 Royal Golden Wedding (printed no.281) 5.00   ☐

1998 Endangered Species (20th January)

Focussing on the plight of six engangered species, from 116 listed in the Biodiversity Action Plan, this pack details their natural habitats and charts their decline.

PP248   1997 Endangered Species (printed no.284) 4.00   ☐

1998 Diana, Princess of Wales (3rd February)

In memory of Diana, Princess of Wales, this pack includes photos of her from early childhood onwards and pays tribute to her enduring human qualities.

PP249

PP249 w

PP249	1998 Diana, Princess of Wales		6.00	☐
w	Welsh language pack	55.00		☐

1998 The Queen's Beasts (24th February)

This pack details the background of The Queen's Beasts, which guarded the entrance to Westminster Abbey during the Coronation, and how the choice of the depicted Arms and Badges was made.

PP250   1998 The Queen's Beasts (printed no.285)   3.50   ☐

1998 Lighthouses (24th March)

In the year when the last manned UK lighthouse became automated, this pack tells the story of Angus Hutchison and his 36 years as a lighthouse-keeper on Fair Isle South, Scotland.

PP251   1998 Lighthouses (printed no.286)   4.00   ☐

1998 Comedians (23rd April)

Commemorating five famous British comedians of the 1960s and 1970s, this pack gives a reminder of their well-known catchphrases and comedic genius.

PP252   1998 Comedians (printed no.287)   5.00   ☐

1998 Health (23rd June)

Celebrating 50 years of the NHS, this pack goes through some of the vast improvements in healthcare since 1948 and lists 10 major medical breakthroughs and discoveries that transformed the health of the nation.

PP253   1998 Health (printed no.288)   3.50   ☐

1998 Magical Worlds (21st July)

Beautifully illustrated by Peter Malone, this colourful pack goes on a journey through the magical worlds of Narnia, The Hobbit and Watership Down, amongst others, that delight children and adults alike.

PP254　1998 Magical Worlds (printed no.289)　5.00　☐

1998 Carnival (25th August)

The Europa theme of 1998 was National Festivals and this pack salutes the Notting Hill Carnival, Britain's greatest multi-cultural festival, with colourful photos and a poem by Benjamin Zephaniah.

PP255　1998 Carnival (printed no.290)　4.00　☐

1998 Speed (29th September)

This pack commemorates the incredible achievements in land speed records of Malcolm Campbell, Henry Seagrave, John G Parry Thomas, John Cobb and Donald Campbell, along with a timeline of each record and archive photos of their 'cars'.

PP256　1998 Speed (printed no.291)　4.00　☐

1998 Christmas Angels (2nd November)

Featuring quotations from prayers and hymns, this pack is designed to be made into a 3D Christmas Angel and contains the instructions to do so.

PP257　1998 Christmas Angels (printed no.292)　4.00　☐

1999 Inventors' Tale (12th January)

The first in a series of 12 'Tales' for 1999, this illustrated pack tells of some of the great British inventions that changed the world, including Harrison's chronometer and Turing's electronic computer.

PP258　1999 Inventors' Tale (printed no.294)　3.75　☐

1999 Travellers' Tale (2nd February)

From the 18th century adventures of Captain Cook to modern-day transatlantic flights, this pack is a reminder of the British men at the forefront of travel.

PP259　1999 Travellers' Tale (printed no.295)　3.75　☐

1999 Patients' Tale (2nd March)

When Edward Jenner developed a vaccination against smallpox, it was a crucial point in the history of medicine. This pack details other similarly crucial work by Alexander Fleming and the founder of nursing care, Florence Nightingale.

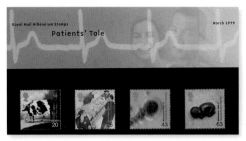

PP260   1999 Patients' Tale (printed no.296)   3.75   ☐

1999 Settlers' Tale (6th April)

Migration, immigration and emigration have all had a profound effect on the British Isles. This pack discusses the impact of people's movement and settlement.

PP261   1999 Settlers' Tale (printed no.297)   3.75   ☐

1999 Workers' Tale (4th May)

From 18th century cotton spinning to the London Stock Exchange, this pack tracks the shift from heavy industry to the electronic workplace.

PP262   1999 Workers' Tale (printed no.298)   3.75   ☐

1999 Entertainers' Tale (1st June)

Featuring photos of many sports, TV, music and film stars, the growth of the entertainment industry is tracked in this pack.

PP263   1999 Enterainers' Tale (printed no.299)   4.00   ☐

1999 The Royal Wedding (15th June)

Commemorating the wedding of HRH Prince Edward to Sophie Rhys-Jones, this pack gives a brief resumé of each and an official engagement photo.

PP264   1999 The Royal Wedding (printed no.M01)   3.00   ☐

1999 Citizens' Tale (6th July)

Development of citizen's Rights began with the Magna Carta but, as this pack describes, much is owed to visionaries Robert Owen and Emmeline Pankhurst for the equal opportunities enjoyed today.

PP265   1999 Citizens' Tale (printed no.300)   3.75   ☐

1999 Scientists' Tale (3rd August)

This illustrated pack features the impact of the great scientists such as Newton, Faraday, Darwin and, more recently, Stephen Hawking.

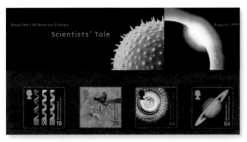

PP266   1999 Scientists' Tale (printed no.301)   3.75   ☐

Also exists as an Error - Silver text missing on cover

1999 Farmers' Tale (7th September)

Agricultural practices saw the English population double between 1180 and 1330 to more than five million. This colourful pack charts the continuing changes that see more machines and fewer farmers.

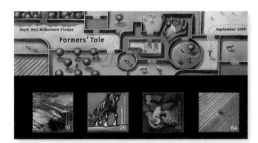

PP267   1999 Farmers' Tale (printed no.302)   3.75   ☐

1999 Soldiers' Tale (5th October)

Full of war-related illustrations and photos, this pack is a reminder of the role of the military throughout British history and the impact of war.

PP268   1999 Soldiers' Tale (printed no.303)   3.75   ☐

1999 Christians' Tale (2nd November)

On the threshold of Christianity's third millennium, this pack tells how religion has been woven into the fabric of social, cultural and political life in Britain.

PP269   1999 Christians' Tale (printed no.304)   3.75   ☐

1999 Artists' Tale (7th December)

This pack celebrates all forms of art and the ability to communicate feelings and emotions through words, music and imagery.

PP270   1999 Artists' Tale (printed no.305)   3.75   ☐

1999 Millennium Timekeeper (14th December)

Marking the new Millennium, the inside of this pack features David Gentleman, designer of the enclosed stamps, discussing the diversity of his work.

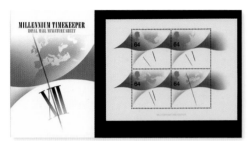

| PP271 | 1999 Millennium Timekeeper (printed no.M02) | 15.00 | ☐ |

2000 Above and Beyond (18th January)

Inspired by Millennium projects throughout the UK, this is the first in a series of 12 packs for 2000. Contains a poem about owls, 'Night Flight from Muncaster' by Jo Shapcott, and discusses the projects featured on the enclosed stamps.

| PP272 | 2000 Above and Beyond (printed no.307) | 3.75 | ☐ |

2000 Fire and Light (1st February)

Inside this pack is a brightly-coloured image and a poem titled 'The Gift of Flame', by John Agard, which encompasses the Millennium projects represented on the enclosed stamps.

| PP273 | 2000 Fire and Light (printed no.308) | 3.75 | ☐ |

2000 Water and Coast (7th March)

Using photography as the basis of its design, the Water and Coast theme of this pack is very evident. Contains a poem, 'Seaham', by Alice Oswald, and discusses the Millennium projects represented on the enclosed stamps.

| PP274 | 2000 Water and Coast (printed no.309) | 3.75 | ☐ |

2000 Life and Earth (4th April)

This pack opens-out to reveal a close-up photo of a curled fern leaf alongside a poem, 'The Lighthouse Keeper's Cat', by Tobias Hill. There is also a description of the four Millennium projects represented on the enclosed stamps.

| PP275 | 2000 Life and Earth (printed no.310) | 3.75 | ☐ |

2000 Art and Craft (2nd May)

The theme of this pack is represented inside by a picture reminiscent of a toolshed and an amusing poem, 'Arts 'n' Crafts' by John Cooper Clarke. There is also a description of the four Millennium projects represented on the enclosed stamps.

| PP276 | 2000 Art and Craft (printed no.311) | 3.75 | ☐ |

2000 Her Majesty's stamps (23rd May)

To mark the production of a new definitive stamp, this pack gives an insight into the design and printing processes used in stamp production.

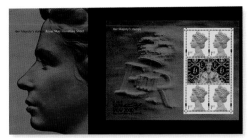

| PP277 | 2000 Her Majesty's stamps (printed no.M03) | 40.00 | ☐ |

2000 People and Place (6th June)

Inside this pack is a poem titled 'The Park Had A Dream', by Moniza Alvi. There is also a description of the four Millennium projects represented on the enclosed stamps.

| PP278 | 2000 People and Place (printed no.312) | 3.75 | ☐ |

2000 Stone and Soil (4th July)

Inside this pack, Strangford Stone, which is one of the Millennium projects represented on the enclosed stamps, is the subject of a poem by Michael Longley. There is also a description of each of the projects.

| PP279 | 2000 Stone and Soil (printed no.313) | 3.75 | ☐ |

2000 Tree and Leaf (1st August)

Highlighting the importance of trees and plants for present and future generations, this pack contains a poem, 'The Hobson Tree', by Holly Ruth Hopkins. There is also a description of the four Millennium projects represented on the enclosed stamps.

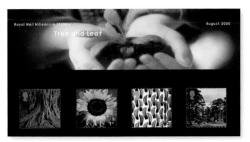

| PP280 | 2000 Tree and Leaf (printed no.314) | 3.75 | ☐ |

2000 100th Year of The Queen Mother (4th August)

Commemorating The Queen Mother's 100th birthday, this pack is full of photos of her through the ages along with a synopsis of her life.

| PP281 | 2000 100th Year of The Queen Mother (printed no.M04) | 16.00 | ☐ |

2000 Mind and Matter (5th September)

Celebrating innovations in technology that enable people to explore the past and look into the future, this pack features a poem titled 'Cast Up', by Lavinia Greenlaw. There is also a description of the four Millennium projects represented on the enclosed stamps.

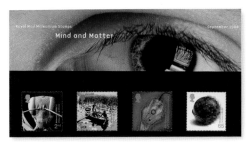

| PP282 | 2000 Mind and Matter (printed no.315) | 3.75 | ☐ |

2000 Body and Bone (3rd October)

The four Millennium projects represented on the enclosed stamps form the basis of this pack, which contains an atmospheric poem by Ian McMillan titled 'The Fat Man in the Bath'.

PP283   2000 Body and Bone (printed no.316)   3.75   ☐

2000 Spirit and Faith (7th November)

In a departure from the usual style of Christmas packs, this one continues the Millennium projects series by opening-out to reveal a poem, 'Eating Chips with the Saints', by David Hart.

PP284   2000 Spirit and Faith (printed no.317)   3.75   ☐

2000 Sound and Vision (5th December)

This pack opens to a bright-colour image and a poem by Carol Ann Duffy titled 'Yes'. There is also a description of the four Millennium projects represented on the enclosed stamps.

PP285   2000 Sound and Vision (printed no.318)   3.75   ☐

2001 Hopes for the Future (16th January)

Concluding Royal Mail's Millennium Collection, this colourful pack focusses on the UN Convention on the Rights of the Child and features the thoughts of Sir Peter Ustinov, UNICEF Goodwill Ambassador.

PP286   2001 Hopes for the Future (printed no.319) 3.75   ☐

2001 Occasions (6th February)

Featuring quotations by Pablo Picasso, Lord Byron and Prince Albert, amongst others, this pack celebrates some special occasions including New Home, New Baby and Birthdays.

PP287   2001 Occasions (printed no.M05)   5.00   ☐

2001 Cats & Dogs (13th February)

This pack includes some endearing black and white photography of our favourite pets and explores the differing relationships between people and their cats and dogs.

PP288   2001 Cats & Dogs (printed no.320)   11.00   ☐

2001 Weather (31st March)

One of the most common topics of British conversation is featured in this illustrated pack, with explanations behind some well-known expressions such as 'raining cats and dogs'.

PP289   2001 Weather (printed no.321)   8.00   ☐

2001 Submarines (10th April)

To commemorate the Centenary of the Royal Navy Submarine Service, this pack contains fascinating facts and figures about life on board HMS Splendid.

PP290   2001 Submarines (printed no.322)   9.50   ☐

2001 Double-Deckers (15th May)

Celebrating the classic British bus, this pack opens-out to reveal a colourful picture of various tickets and a leaflet that contains the technical specifications of 16 buses, dating from 1908 to 1999.

PP291   2001 Double-Deckers (printed no.323)   8.00   ☐

2001 Fabulous Hats (19th June)

This stylish, colourful pack describes the work of four eminent British milliners; Pip Hackett, Dai Rees, Stephen Jones and Philip Treacy.

PP292   2001 Fabulous Hats (printed no.324)   6.00   ☐

2001 Pond Life (10th July)

Four familiar pond species are featured in this pack with a synopsis of each, including the common frog, great diving beetle, three-spined stickleback and southern hawker dragonfly. Other pond life, above and below the water, is also illustrated.

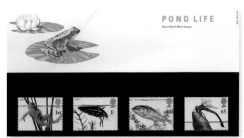

PP293   2001 Pond Life (printed no.325)   6.00   ☐

2001 Punch & Judy (4th September)

This lavish pack opens to reveal a fully illustrated Punch & Judy tent, complete with a push-out section to create the 'stage'. There's also an excerpt from 'Interview with a Punchman' written by Henry Mayhew in 1851.

PP294   2001 Punch & Judy (printed no.326)   6.00   ☐

2001 Nobel Prizes (2nd October)

Marking the Centenary of the Nobel Prizes, this pack features six previous winners each giving their thoughts on one of the six Prize categories. There is also a list of all the UK winners up to 2001.

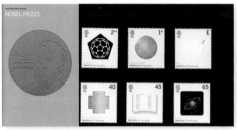

PP295   2001 Nobel Prizes (printed no.327)   24.00   ☐

2001 Flags & Ensigns (22nd October)

This pack explains the design and usage of the flags and ensigns featured on the enclosed stamps. Inside, Commander Jeremy Nash of HMS Proteus recounts a night on patrol in 1942.

PP296   2001 Flags & Ensigns (printed no.M06)   18.00   ☐

2001 Christmas (6th November)

Fully illustrated by Arthur Robins, this pack opens-out to create an amusing board game based on the territorial rivalry of robins in the garden.

PP297   2001 Christmas (printed no.328)   6.00   ☐

2002 Rudyard Kipling (15th January)

Commemorating 100 years since publication of his 'Just So Stories', this wonderfully-illustrated pack features a poem and discusses Kipling's unique use of language, repetition and myth.

PP298   2002 Rudyard Kipling (printed no.330)   12.50   ☐

2002 The Golden Jubilee (6th February)

In celebration of the 50th Anniversary of The Queen's accession to the throne, this pack simply contains extracts from seven of her messages and speeches spanning the fifty years.

PP299   2002 The Golden Jubilee (printed no.331)   8.00   ☐

2002 Occasions (5th March)

Marking happy occasions and special events, inside this pack is a photo of a fridge door with memos and notes pinned to it.

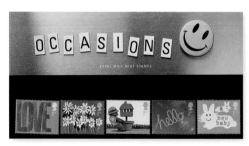

PP300   2002 Occasions (printed no.M07)   6.00   ☐

2002 Coastlines (19th March)

This attractive pack opens to reveal colour illustrations, by Jane Human, of three coastal scenes; Blyth in Northumberland, Robin Hood's Bay in North Yorkshire, Dunstanburgh Castle in Northumberland. There are also some interesting facts and figures about Britain's 7,000-mile coastline.

PP301   2002 Coastlines (printed no.332)   6.00   ☐

2002 Circus (10th April)

Commonly dubbed 'The Greatest Show on Earth', circuses began as a trick horse-riding exhibition in London. This pack delves into the story behind the stars of the Big Top.

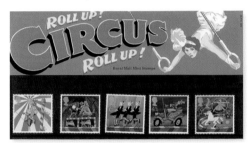

PP302   2002 Circus (printed no.333)   6.00   ☐

2002 HM The Queen Mother (25th April)

In memory of The Queen Mother, this pack contains a simple montage of black and white photos of her, aged 2 to 95.

PP303   2002 HM The Queen Mother
(printed no.M08)   6.00   ☐

2002 Airliners (2nd May)

Commemorating 50 years of passenger jet service, this pack looks at the development of airliners and changes in travel. Includes some archive photos of first-class cabins and stewardesses.

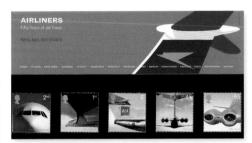

PP304   2002 Airliners (printed no.334)   8.00   ☐

2002 World Cup (21st May)

Issued in advance of the football World Cup, this pack looks back at how the England team qualified and anticipates their success in Korea. Features quotes by David Beckham and Sven-Göran Eriksson.

PP305   2002 World Cup (printed no.335)   5.50   ☐

2002 The Friendly Games (16th July)

The 17th Commonwealth Games, held in Manchester, were the first to incorporate able-bodied and disabled athletes in parallel competition. This pack features four young athletes looking to make their mark.

PP306   2002 The Friendly Games (printed no.336) 6.00   ☐

2002 Peter Pan (20th August)

This pack celebrates the magical story of The Boy Who Wouldn't Grow Up and author James Matthew Barrie, who left the copyright of Peter Pan to Great Ormond Street Hospital. Contains pictures and illustrations of stage productions and various memorabilia.

PP307   2002 Peter Pan (printed no.337)   7.50   □

2002 The Bridges of London (10th September)

This pack tells the interesting story of Old London Bridge and the life that flowed over and under it, from construction c. 1176-1209 to its replacement in 1831. There is also an aerial photo showing the location of today's Thames bridges.

PP308   2002 The Bridges of London
(printed no.338)   24.00   □

2002 Astronomy (24th September)

Inside this pack is a representation of the night sky, showing the five major circumpolar constellations and a guide to the stars. There is also brief mention of William Herschel's discovery of planetary nebula.

PP309   2002 Astronomy (printed no.339)   7.50   □

2002 Pillar to Post (8th October)

Celebrating the 150th Anniversary of Britain's first pillar letter boxes, this pack gives their history from humble beginnings in the Channel Islands. There is also a pictorial list of pillar box designs from 1852 to 1968 and corresponding Royal cyphers.

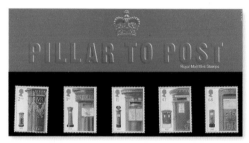

PP310   2002 Pillar to Post (printed no.340)   6.00   □

2002 Christmas (5th November)

This pack discusses the ritual use of evergreens in homes and churches at Christmas time and the symbolism of ivy, holly, mistletoe, fir and cones.

PP311   2002 Christmas (printed no.341)   6.00   □

2003 Birds of Prey (14th January)

Featuring the barn owl and kestrel, this pack opens to a photo of each and details their habitats, hunting and breeding patterns. There is also a reminder of the importance of their conservation.

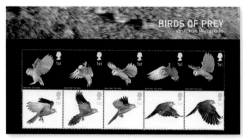

PP312   2003 Birds of Prey (printed no.343)   11.00   □

2003 Occasions (4th February)

Fully illustrated by Steven Appleby and based on the theme of the enclosed stamps, this pack opens-out into an amusing multiple-choice game and a cartoon 'training' course in correspondence.

Inside the pack is a multiple-choice game

PP313   2003 Occasions (printed no.M09)   8.00   ☐

2003 The Secret of Life (25th February)

In the 50 years after Crick and Watson discovered the structure of DNA, the Human Genome Project came a long way. This pack takes the form of questions and answers to help explain some of the research and conclusions drawn.

PP314   2003 The Secret of Life (printed no.344)   7.00   ☐

2003 Fun Fruit and Veg (25th March)

Illustrated by Jason Ford, inside this pack is a cartoon of fruit and veg plotting their escape from a supermarket with the aid of disguises. This is all based around the enclosed stamps and sticky labels provided to attach to them.

PP315   2003 Fun Fruit and Veg (printed no.345)   15.00   ☐

2003 Extreme Endeavours (29th April)

Commemorating the 50th Anniversary of Hillary and Tenzing's conquer of Everest, this pack tells of some of the great British explorers, with a focus on the expeditions of Sir Ranulph Fiennes and Rebecca Stephens.

PP316   2003 Extreme Endeavours (printed no.346)   7.00   ☐

2003 The Coronation (2nd June)

Containing details of The Queen's Coronation ceremony, Crown Jewels and regalia, this pack includes photos of her arriving at Westminster Abbey and of the moment of Coronation.

PP317   2003 The Coronation (printed no.347)   12.00   ☐

2003 HRH Prince William (17th June)

In celebration of Prince William's 21st birthday, this pack features 21 photos of him from babyhood in 1982 to adulthood in 2002. It also shows his Coat of Arms which includes a small sea shell derived from his mother's family Arms. Written in English and Welsh.

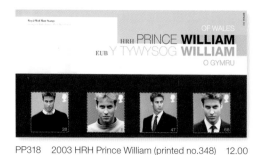

PP318   2003 HRH Prince William (printed no.348)   12.00   ☐

2003 Scotland (15th July)

Celebrating all things Scottish, this pack is full of facts, figures and photos that represent the history and diversity of the country.

PP319   2003 Scotland (printed no.349)   7.00   ☐

2003 Pub Signs (12th August)

Since 1393, it has been compulsory for alehouses to exhibit a sign. With colour images throughout, this pack takes a look at some of the most popular pub names and their derivation.

PP320   2003 Pub Signs (printed no.350)   7.00   ☐

2003 Transports of Delight (18th September)

Designed in a retro style reflecting the subject matter, this pack features the most popular British toys from the 'golden age' of production including Hornby, Dinky and Meccano. There is also a collector's guide and estimated market values.

PP321   2003 Transports of Delight (printed no.351)   7.00   ☐

2003 The British Museum (7th October)

Marking 250 years of The British Museum, this pack contains pictures of fascinating artefacts and treasures from the collection, along with Sir David Attenborough's experience of it.

PP322   2003 The British Museum (printed no.352)   7.00   ☐

2003 Christmas (4th November)

Featuring the work of Andy Goldsworthy, this pack contains photos of his dramatic sculptures and details how he created them.

PP323   2003 Christmas (printed no.353)   7.00   ☐

2003 England Winners (19th December)

Celebrating England's Rugby World Cup victory over Australia, this pack lists the winning team statistics and opens to an illustration representing the state of play in the final seconds, as Jonny Wilkinson kicked the winning goal.

PP324   2003 England Winners (printed no.M9B)   12.00   ☐

2004 Classic Locomotives (13th January)

Containing illustrations and technical specifications of six classic steam locomotives, this pack discusses the railways they ran on, the way they were utilised and their preservation.

PP325   2004 Classic Locomotives (printed no.355) 9.00   ☐

2004 Occasions (3rd February)

Illustrated throughout by Satoshi Kambayashi, this pack opens to reveal a fun board game.

The pack is also a fun board game

PP326   2004 Occasions (printed no.M10A)   3.90   ☐

2004 The Lord of The Rings (26th February)

In tribute to the author JRR Tolkien, this pack provides a resumé of his life and discusses the inspiration behind his epic tale The Lord of the Rings. Inside is designed in the style of a book.

PP327   2004 The Lord of The Rings
         (printed no.356))   14.00   ☐

2004 Northern Ireland (16th March)

Celebrating Northern Ireland, this pack is full of facts, figures and photos that represent the landscape, history and diversity of the country.

PP328   2004 Northern Ireland (printed no.357)   7.00   ☐

2004 Entente Cordiale (6th April)

Marking a century of the 'Friendly Understanding', this pack tells the history behind it and looks at some modern Franco-British collaborations.

PP329   2004 Entente Cordiale (printed no.358)   15.00   ☐

2004 Ocean Liners (13th April)

The original transatlantic liners are celebrated in this pack which features a dramatic photo of the launching ceremony for Mauretania II in 1938, plus pictures and information about the universally admired Queen Mary.

PP330   2004 Ocean Liners (printed no.359)   7.00   ☐

2004 Royal Horticultural Society (25th May)

Commemorating the Bicentenary of the RHS, this beautifully-illustrated pack features six plants that play an important part in garden history. There is also a timeline of the Society's history.

PP331   2004 Royal Horticultural Society
(printed no.360)   7.00   ☐

2004 Wales (15th June)

Celebrating all things Welsh, this pack is full of facts, figures and photos that represent the rich history, traditions and diversity of the country. Written in English and Welsh.

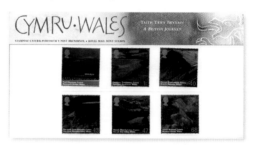

PP332   2004 Wales (printed no.361)   7.00   ☐

2004 RSA (10th August)

To mark the 250th year of the RSA, this pack highlights some of their key initiatives for the future and points out some of their past campaigns and achievements. There is also a timeline of the Society's history.

PP333   2004 RSA (printed no.362)   7.00   ☐

2004 Woodland Animals (16th September)

In this pack, Bill Oddie discusses the 10 woodland animals that are featured on the enclosed stamps. The pack opens to reveal an image of a woodland scene on each side, with photos and descriptions of the animals.

PP334   2004 Woodland Animals (printed no.363)   11.00   ☐

2004 The Crimean War (12th October)

150 years on from the start of the Crimean War, this pack contains a synopsis of the Battles, evocative archive photos and a report by war correspondent William Howard Russell. It also includes 'The Charge of the Light Brigade' by Alfred, Lord Tennyson.

PP335   2004 The Crimean War (printed no.364)   7.00   ☐

2004 Christmas (2nd November)

Fully illustrated by Raymond Briggs, this pack opens-out into a cartoon strip of Father Christmas performing his duties. It also tells the story behind the character and of Briggs' other much-loved books.

PP336   2004 Christmas (printed no.365)   7.00   ☐

2005 Farm Animals (11th January)

This pack looks at a year in the life of a smallholder, with details of the changing workload through the seasons plus photos of traditional British livestock and their uses.

PP337   2005 Farm Animals (printed no.367)   11.00   ☐

2005 South West England (8th February)

Alongside photos of the landscape, this pack goes on a journey through the West country, from Marlborough in Wiltshire to Land's End, including details of Stonehenge, Bath's Royal Crescent, Glastonbury and The Eden Project.

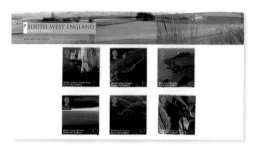

PP338   2005 South West England (printed no.368)   7.00   ☐

2005 Jane Eyre (24th February)

Celebrating the most famous of Charlotte Brontë's novels, this pack includes quotations and illustrations from early editions, along with a synopsis of the story.

PP339   2005 Jane Eyre (printed no.369)   8.00   ☐

2005 Magic (15th March)

Commemorating the Centenary of The Magic Circle, this pack features past and present masters of magic and their trademark tricks. There is also a photo of 10 most common 'tools' of the trade, compiled in the form of a Magic Set.

PP340   2005 Magic (printed no.370)   8.00   ☐

2005 Royal Wedding (8th April)

To mark the occasion of the marriage of HRH The Prince of Wales to Camilla Parker Bowles, this pack simply contains brief details of their engagement and two photos of the couple. Written in English and Welsh.

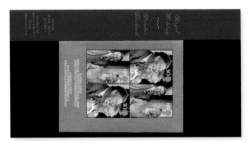

PP341   2005 Royal Wedding (printed no.M10)   8.00   ☐

2005 World Heritage Sites (21st April)

Featuring attractive photography throughout, this pack explains how a Site is considered for the World Heritage List and contains a list of the 26 Sites established in the UK and Overseas Territories, with a focus on five of them.

PP342   2005 World Heritage Sites (printed no.371) 8.00   ☐

2005 Trooping The Colour (7th June)

Written by HRH The Duke of Edinburgh, this colourful pack details the history of Trooping the Colour and includes photos of the Guards' uniform emblems, which help distinguish the various regiments.

PP343   2005 Trooping The Colour (printed no.372) 8.00   ☐

2005 Motorcycles (19th July)

Taking a fond look at some of the best British motorcycles, this pack details those featured on the enclosed stamps and discusses production rise and fall from the First World War to 2005. With accompanying photos.

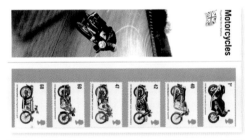

PP344   2005 Motorcycles (printed no.373)   10.00   ☐

2005 London 2012 Host City (5th August)

This pack simply comprises a photo of the celebrations as the announcement was made that London would host the 2012 Olympics and Paralympics.

PP345   2005 London 2012 Host City
         (printed no.M11)   10.00   ☐

2005 Changing Tastes in Britain (23rd August)

Written by chef Keith Floyd, this pack highlights the dramatic increase in food choices since the Second World War and the flavours that are now taken for granted.

| PP346 | 2005 Changing Tastes in Britain (printed no.374) | 7.50 | ☐ |

2005 Classic ITV (15th September)

Commemorating 50 years of ITV, this pack charts the rise of commercial television, with archive stills from some of the biggest shows and programme listings divided into the four main genres, shown in the style of a TV guide.

| PP347 | 2005 Classic ITV (printed no.375) | 7.00 | ☐ |

2005 The Ashes (6th October)

Celebrating England's first Ashes win for 16 years, this pack gives all the facts and figures of each of the five Test matches, plus player statistics.

| PP348 | 2005 The Ashes (printed no.M12) | 7.00 | ☐ |

2005 Trafalgar (18th October)

To commemorate the 200th Anniversary of the Battle of Trafalgar, this pack contains a wealth of information about life on board the Victory, Nelson's battle tactics and the establishment of a British global order.

| PP349 | 2005 Trafalgar (printed no.376) | 7.00 | ☐ |

2005 Christmas (1st November)

The theme of this pack is the image of Madonna & Child and it discusses the wide variety of interpretations, along with pictures of some famous artworks.

| PP350 | 2005 Christmas (printed no.377) | 7.00 | ☐ |

2006 Animal Tales (10th January)

Celebrating the world of children's books, this colourful pack contains amusing poems by Roger McGough, fully illustrated by Sara Fanelli.

| PP351 | 2006 Animal Tales (printed no.379) | 9.00 | ☐ |

2006 England (7th February)

Alongside photos of beautiful landscapes, this pack goes on a journey through England, from the North Downs Way to the Midlands, before heading north to Carlisle.

PP352   2006 England (printed no.380)   7.00   ☐

2006 Isambard Kingdom Brunel (23rd February)

Marking the 200th Anniversary of the birth of Brunel, the most innovative engineer of his time, this pack features photos and details of five of his most outstanding designs; SS Great Britain, Paddington Station, Royal Albert Bridge, Maidenhead Bridge and Clifton Suspension Bridge.

PP353   2006 Isambard Kingdom Brunel
         (printed no.381)   7.00   ☐

2006 Ice Age Animals (21st March)

This pack gives a fascinating insight into animal life in Ice Age Britain, with details of the five animals featured on the enclosed stamps. It also contains photos of the excavations and findings at Stanton Harcourt, near Oxford.

PP354   2006 Ice Age Animals (printed no.382)   7.00   ☐

2006 HM The Queen's 80th Birthday (18th April)

Packed with over 80 photos of The Queen, this pack gives a synopsis of her life.

PP355   2006 HM The Queen's 80th Birthday
         (printed no.383)   9.00   ☐

2006 World Cup Winners (6th June)

Featuring six winning countries of the Football World Cup, this pack contains statistics, facts and figures from previous Finals, plus photos of some of the most famous players.

PP356   2006 World Cup Winners (printed no.384)   8.50   ☐

2006 Modern Architecture (20th June)

Celebrating the wonder of modern buildings, this pack studies the evolution of architectural design and features photos of the Eden Project, The Deep and the Selfridges building in Birmingham.

PP357   2006 Modern Architecture (printed no.385)   7.00   ☐

2006 National Portrait Gallery (18th July)

In celebration of 150 years since the founding of the Gallery, this pack tells of the principles and policies that determine its collection. There are also photos of some of the portraits.

| PP358 | 2006 National Portrait Gallery (printed no.386) | 9.00 | ☐ |

2006 Victoria Cross (21st September)

Marking 150 years of the Victoria Cross, this pack presents stories of valour by General Sir Peter de la Billière, along with illustrations, photos and images of newspaper cuttings featuring 12 courageous recipients.

| PP359 | 2006 Victoria Cross (printed no.387) | 9.00 | ☐ |

2006 Sounds of Britain (3rd October)

This illustrated pack looks at the impact that modern music has had on British culture, from the 'imported' calypso of Trinidad, to the punk of London.

| PP360 | 2006 Sounds of Britain (printed no.388) | 8.00 | ☐ |

2006 Smilers (17th October)

This pack opens to reveal an illustration that represents the occasions on which the enclosed stamps might be used.

| PP361 | 2006 Smilers (printed no.M13) | 14.00 | ☐ |

2006 Christmas (7th November)

Written by Leah Moore, this fully illustrated pack contains a Christmas tale for children.

| PP362 | 2006 Christmas (printed no.389) | 9.00 | ☐ |

2006 Lest we forget (9th November)

Recounting the Battle of the Somme, this pack contains archive photos and focusses on the Accrington Pals battalion. The inside simply features the poem 'In Flanders Fields'.

| PP363 | 2006 Lest we forget (printed no.390) | 7.50 | ☐ |

2006 Celebrating Scotland (30th November)

Featuring photos that typify the country and quotes by famous Scots throughout, this pack commemorates St Andrew's Day and tells the legend of how his bones were taken to Scotland.

PP364   2006 Celebrating Scotland (printed no.M14)   6.00   ☐

2007 The Beatles (9th January)

To mark 50 years since Lennon and McCartney first met, this pack follows the prolific career of the 'Fab Four' and notes their undoubted impact on popular culture. Contains images of album sleeves and memorabilia. **Note:** An additional minisheet of stamps is included in the back of the pack.

PP365   2007 The Beatles (printed no.392)   14.00   ☐

2007 Sea Life (1st February)

The coasts of Britain foster a wealth of species and this pack gives information about various crustaceans, fish and mammals that rely on the marine environment.

PP366   2007 Sea Life (printed no.393)   9.00   ☐

2007 The Sky at Night (13th February)

Celebrating 50 years of TV programme 'The Sky at Night', and written by Patrick Moore, this pack features pictures of astronomical interest and tells of his 'C' number system.

PP367   2007 The Sky at Night (printed no.394)   8.00   ☐

2007 World of Invention (1st March)

Fully illustrated by Peter Till, the inside of this pack resembles a sketch pad of ideas for invention, while the back contains information about 12 of the most influential British inventors and their designs.

PP368   2007 World of Invention (printed no.395)   8.00   ☐

2007 Abolition of the Slave Trade (22nd March)

Commemorating the Bicentenary of the abolition of the Slave Trade in 1807, this pack highlights the long-fought campaign that began 20 years earlier. Contains details of the six abolitionists featured on the enclosed stamps and illustrations of slavery.

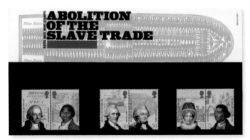

PP369   2007 Abolition of the Slave Trade
(printed no.396)   8.00   ☐

2007 Celebrating England (23rd April)

Featuring photos that typify the country and quotes by famous Englishmen throughout, this pack commemorates St George's Day and tells of his rather anonymous beginnings.

PP370   2007 Celebrating England (printed no.M15)   7.00   ☐

2007 Beside the Seaside (15th May)

Celebrating the original family holiday, this pack takes an affectionate look at the Great British seaside through the eyes of travel writer Simon Calder.

PP371   2007 Beside the Seaside (printed no.397)   8.00   ☐

2007 Machin Definitives 40th Anniversary

(5th June)
In tribute to Arnold Machin, revered sculptor and creator of the image of The Queen on all definitive stamps since 1967, this pack gives a synopsis of his life and contains images of some of his other works.

PP372   2007 Machin Definitives 40th Anniversary
(printed no.398)   8.00   ☐

2007 Grand Prix (3rd July)

This pack focusses on Stirling Moss, one of the great British racing drivers, with statistics, photos and his own thoughts on motor racing. There are also statistics and photos of five other 'greats'; Graham Hill, Jim Clark, Jackie Stewart, James Hunt and Nigel Mansell.

PP373   2007 Grand Prix (printed no.399)   8.00   ☐

2007 Harry Potter (17th July)

Designed in the style of a satchel, this pack opens to look like Harry Potter's school desk might appear and charts the rise in popularity of J.K. Rowling's books and their indelible mark on British culture. **Note:** An additional minisheet of stamps is included in the back of the pack.

PP374   2007 Harry Potter (printed no.M16)   14.00   ☐

2007 Scout Centenary (26th July)

Marking 100 years of Scouting, which was celebrated in the UK at the 21st World Scout Jamboree, this pack discusses all aspects of this worldwide movement. With information, photos and quotes from famous Scouts such as Richard Branson and Ray Mears.

PP375   2007 Scout Centenary (printed no.400)   7.50   ☐

2007 Birds (4th September)

Written by Tony Soper, this pack looks at the impact of habitat management and farming practices on the recovery and protection of British bird species. Contains details of the 10 birds featured on the enclosed stamps.

PP376   2007 Birds (printed no.401)   12.50   ☐

2007 British Army Uniforms (20th September)

This pack opens to reveal a colour illustration of a Rifleman of the 95th Regiment c. 1813, with specific details of his uniform. Seven modern uniforms are also represented, with information as to the relevance of colour and pattern.

PP377   2007 British Army Uniforms (printed no.402) 9.00   ☐

2007 Diamond Wedding Anniversary
(16th October)

In celebration of the Royal Diamond Wedding Anniversary, this pack contains a montage of images relating to the Wedding day plus details of the wedding dress, the cake and the ring.
Note: An additional minisheet of stamps is included in the back of the pack.

PP378   2007 Diamond Wedding Anniversary
         (printed no.403)   13.00   ☐

2007 Christmas (6th November)

Starting with the history behind 'Hark the Herald Angels Sing', one of the best loved Christmas carols, this pack then discusses the nature of 'angels', our relationship with them and how they are depicted.

PP379   2007 Christmas (printed no.404)   11.00   ☐

2007 Lest we forget (8th November)

Recounting the Third Battle of Ypres, this pack focusses on the fall of Passchendaele. Contains archive photos, facts and figures, and the poem 'Passchendaele' by present-day war poet S.J. Robinson.

PP380   2007 Lest we forget (printed no.405)   8.00   ☐

2008 James Bond (8th January)

Commemorating the Centenary of the birth of Ian Fleming, this lavishly illustrated pack looks at the similarities between his own life and that of his greatest character James Bond, in the form of a timeline.

PP381   2008 James Bond (printed no.407)   12.00   ☐

2008 Working Dogs (5th February)

Celebrating man's best friend, this pack looks at working dogs' role in supporting and helping their two-legged companions. Details typical breeds, tasks and skills, of guide dogs, assistance dogs, sheepdogs, and those in the police, customs and mountain rescue.

PP382   2008 Working Dogs (printed no.408)   8.00   ☐

2008 The Houses of Lancaster and York

(28th February)
Illustrated with battle scenes, this pack looks at the dynastic conflict of the Wars of The Roses, and the Hundred Years War which actually lasted 116 years. There are also details of the six kings featured on the enclosed stamps. **Note:** An additional minisheet of stamps is included in the back of the pack.

PP383   2008 The Houses of Lancaster and York
(printed no.409)   8.00   ☐

2008 Celebrating Northern Ireland (11th March)

Featuring photos that typify the country and quotes about Ireland throughout, this pack commemorates St Patrick's Day.

PP384   2008 Celebrating Northern Ireland
(printed no.410)   7.00   ☐

2008 Mayday. Rescue at Sea (13th March)

This pack opens into a fully illustrated 'cartoon' of an imaginary rescue at sea. It also gives details of the Maritime & Coastguard Agency (MCA) and the lifeboats of the RNLI, plus images of 12 maritime distress signals.

PP385   2008 Mayday. Rescue at Sea
(printed no.411)   7.00   ☐

2008 Insects (15th April)

Full of close-up photos of some of Britain's rare and endangered insects, this pack focusses on the species featured on the enclosed stamps and the importance of their conservation.

PP386   2008 Insects (printed no.412)   9.00   ☐

2008 Cathedrals (13th May)

Celebrating six of the most awe-inspiring cathedrals in Britain, this pack features plan drawings and some details of their history, alongside photos of the beautiful interiors. **Note:** An additional minisheet of stamps is included in the back of the pack.

PP387   2008 Cathedrals (printed no.413)   14.00   ☐

2008 Carry On and Hammer films (10th June)

Commemorating 50 years of Carry On Comedy and Hammer Horror, this pack romps through the film titles that became synonymous with childish vulgarity and blood stained shirts. Contains film stills and faux advertising posters.

PP388   2008 Carry On and Hammer films
(printed no.414)   9.00   ☐

2008 Air Displays (17th July)

Marking the 100th Anniversary of Samuel Cody's ground-breaking flight at Farnborough, this pack focusses on the story of aviation as entertainment. Contains archive photos of aircraft and air displays around the country, along with a timeline of aviation history since 1908.

PP389   2008 Air Displays (printed no.415)   8.00   ☐

2008 Olympic Games (22nd August)

Whilst looking forward to London 2012, this pack's focus is the achievements of 10 British medal winners in previous Olympic Games, from Harold Abrahams in 1924 to Dame Kelly Holmes in 2004. Contains photos of the athletes and lists other Olympic records.

PP390   2008 Olympic Games (printed no.M17)   25.00   ☐

2008 RAF Uniforms (18th September)

Tracing the development of RAF uniforms, this pack is full of illustrative photos of service men through the years, along with some examples of their own nicknames for parts of their kit.

PP391   2008 RAF Uniforms (printed no.416)   8.00   ☐

2008 Women of Distinction (14th October)

Honouring six remarkable women, this pack tells the stories of those featured on the enclosed stamps whose steely determination in fighting for their causes changed the lives of all women forever.

PP392   2008 Women of Distinction (printed no.417) 8.00   ☐

2008 Christmas (4th November)

A celebration of music, dance and slapstick comedy, Pantomime remains popular in the 21st century. This colourful pack is full of photos of the typical goodies and baddies and details their roles.

PP393   2008 Christmas (printed no.418)   8.00   ☐

2008 Lest we forget (6th November)

Recounting the end of the Great War, this pack tells how Germany negotiated the ceasefire that subsequently led to Armistice Day. Contains archive photos, facts and figures, and the poem 'Armistice Day' by Tony Channing.

PP394   2008 Lest we forget (printed no.419)   8.00   ☐

2009 British Design Classics (13th January)

Containing modern and archive photos, this pack features 10 iconic pieces of design that have each, in their own way, contributed to British cultural history.

PP395   2009 British Design Classics
(printed no.421)   14.00   ☐

2009 Robert Burns (22nd January)

Commemorating the 250th Anniversary of the birth of Robert Burns, this pack gives a synopsis of his life and contains one of his most famous songs 'A Man's A Man For A' That'.

PP396   2009 Robert Burns (printed no.422)   8.00   ☐

2009 Darwin (12th February)

200 years since his birth and 150 years since publication of his ground-breaking book 'On the Origin of Species', this pack contains photos and information about Darwin's theories and what influenced him. **Note:** An additional minisheet of stamps is included in the back of the pack.

PP397   2009 Darwin (printed no.423)   12.00   ☐

2009 Celebrating Wales (26th February)

Featuring photos that typify the country and quotes by famous Welshmen throughout, this pack commemorates St David's Day and tells of typical celebrations.

PP398   2009 Celebrating Wales (printed no.424)   7.00   ☐

2009 Pioneers of the Industrial Revolution
(10th March)

Full of information and illustrations, this pack tells the story of the Industrial Revolution, particularly the individual contributions of members of the Lunar Society, which included Charles Darwin's grandfathers.

PP399   2009 Pioneers of the Industrial Revolution
(printed no.425)   9.00   ☐

2009 The House of Tudor (21st April)

This pack looks at the turbulent reign of the six Tudor monarchs, encompassing religious change, creation of the first theatres and growth of a dominant naval power. **Note:** An additional minisheet of stamps is included in the back of the pack.

PP400   2009 The House of Tudor (printed no.426)   12.00   ☐

2009 Plants (19th May)

Fully illustrated throughout with colour drawings supplied by Kew Gardens, this pack tells of the decline in Britain's wild plants, with a focus on the 10 endangered species featured on the enclosed stamps. **Note:** An additional minisheet of stamps is included in the back of the pack.

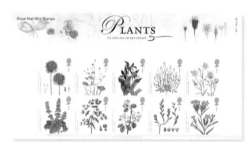

PP401   2009 Plants (printed no.427)   14.00   ☐

2009 Mythical Creatures (16th June)

This pack is fully illustrated, by Dave McKean, with mythical creatures of legends and fairy tales, and it tells the imaginary story behind each one.

PP402   2009 Mythical Creatures (printed no.428)   9.00   ☐

2009 Post Boxes (18th August)

Full of photos of post boxes old and modern, this pack tells the history of their development and features an illustrated timeline of post box design from 1809 to 1995.

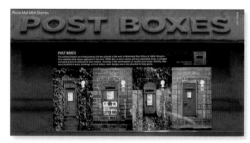

PP403   2009 Post Boxes (printed no.430)   7.00   ☐

2009 Fire and Rescue Service (1st September)

In honour of the brave members of the Fire and Rescue Service, this pack details a typical shift at a fire station and describes some of the types of incident they might tackle.

PP404   2009 Fire and Rescue Service (printed no.429)   10.00   ☐

2009 Royal Navy Uniforms (17th September)

Tracing the development of Royal Navy uniform design, this pack contains illustrative photos of service men in practical modern dress and images of early naval dress by comparison.

PP405   2009 Royal Navy Uniforms (printed no.431)   9.00   ☐

2009 Eminent Britons (8th October)

Featuring the 10 eminent Britons illustrated on the enclosed stamps, this pack tells the stories of their lives.

PP406   2009 Eminent Britons (printed no.432)   10.00   □

2009 Olympic & Paralympic Games (22nd October)

This brightly-coloured pack details 10 sports of the Olympic & Paralympic Games and some of the disciplines within them.

PP407   2009 Olympic & Paralympic Games
(printed no.M18)   11.00   □

2009 Christmas (3rd November)

The theme of this Christmas pack is 'stained glass' and it tells the history of its use from 1st century AD to the modern age; accompanied by colour images of stained glass panels.

PP408   2009 Christmas (printed no.433)   9.50   □

2010 Classic Album Covers (7th January)

In evidence of the saying 'every picture tells a story', this pack looks at those behind the album covers featured on the enclosed stamps, as well as the company Hipgnosis who created many distinctive designs.

PP409   2010 Classic Album Covers (printed no.435)   14.00   □

2010 Smilers, business & consumer (26th January)

This pack opens to reveal two illustrations that tie-in with the enclosed stamps.

PP410   2010 Smilers, business & consumer
(printed no.M19)   14.00   □

2010 Girlguiding UK Centenary (2nd February)

Commemorating 100 years of Girlguiding, this pack describes the activities and aims of the Rainbows, Brownies, Guides and Senior Section members, and contains photos of them in action.

PP411   2010 Girlguiding UK Centenary
(printed no.436)   7.00   □

2010 The Royal Society (25th February)

To mark 350 years of The Royal Society, this pack features the work of the 10 Fellows featured on the enclosed stamps, with a synopsis and accompanying image for each.

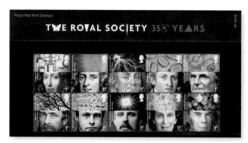

| PP412 | 2010 The Royal Society (printed no.437) | 12.00 | ☐ |

2010 Battersea Dogs & Cats Home (11th March)

Commemorating the 150th Anniversary of Battersea Dogs & Cats Home this pack tells its story, with accompanying photos, and looks behind the scenes at the vital care provided. There is also a timeline of its history.

| PP413 | 2010 Battersea Dogs & Cats Home (printed no.438) | 12.50 | ☐ |

2010 The House of Stewart (23rd March)

This pack looks at one of the longest-lasting dynasties in Europe with details of the seven monarchs. There is also information about Scotland's cultural renaissance and academic evolution during their reigns. **Note:** An additional minisheet of stamps is included in the back of the pack.

| PP414 | 2010 The House of Stewart (printed no.439) | 12.00 | ☐ |

2010 Mammals (13th April)

In recognition of the International Year of Biodiversity, this pack profiles 10 of Britain's mammals that face an uncertain future. Contains illustrations plus facts and figures for each animal.

| PP415 | 2010 Mammals (printed no.440) | 9.00 | ☐ |

2010 George V Accession (8th May)

Commemorating the Centenary of the accession of King George V, this pack is full of information about the design and production of his stamps. Contains many detailed illustrations and images of original drawings, dies and proofs. **Note:** An additional minisheet of stamps is included in the back of the pack.

| PP416 | 2010 George V Accession (printed no.441) | 11.00 | ☐ |

2010 Britain Alone (13th May)

This pack is a reminder of the extraordinary efforts of the ordinary people of Britain during World War II. Contains evocative archive photos and quotations from Winston Churchill's rallying broadcasts. **Note:** An additional minisheet of stamps is included in the back of the pack.

| PP417 | 2010 Britain Alone (printed no.442) | 15.00 | ☐ |

2010 The House of Stuart (15th June)

This pack looks at the royal House of Stuart and the religious tensions that dominated during their reigns. Contains images of artworks that depict some of the most notable events.
Note: An additional minisheet of stamps is included in the back of the pack.

PP418   2010 The House of Stuart (printed no.443)   12.00   ☐

2010 Olympic & Paralympic Games (27th July)

Fully illustrated, this pack contains facts and figures about the 10 sports featured on the enclosed stamps and some of the disciplines within them.

PP419   2010 Olympic & Paralympic Games
(printed no.444)   10.00   ☐

2010 Great British Railways (19th August)

Celebrating Britain's much-loved steam locomotives, this pack focusses on the period from 1923, when the Big Four was formed, to the mid-60's and the end of the steam era. Contains photos, memorabilia and facts and figures on locomotives.

PP420   2010 Great British Railways
(printed no.445)   8.00   ☐

2010 Medical Breakthroughs (16th September)

Looking at six of the most important medical breakthroughs of the 19th and 20th centuries, this pack illustrates each one and tells of the people behind them.

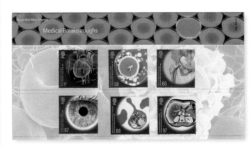

PP421   2010 Medical Breakthroughs
(printed no.446)   8.00   ☐

2010 Winnie the Pooh (12th October)

90 years after the birth of Christopher Robin Milne, this pack tells the story of how he and his favourite teddy bear became the subjects of some of the best-loved classics of children's literature. Contains illustrations by E.H. Shepard. **Note:** An additional minisheet of stamps is included in the back of the pack.

PP422   2010 Winnie the Pooh (printed no.447)   13.00   ☐

2010 Christmas (2nd November)

This delightful pack opens to reveal a picture of Wallace & Gromit that is designed to be used as an advent calendar. The back shows festive images of the duo preparing for Christmas.

Inside the pack is an advent calendar

PP423   2010 Christmas (printed no.448)   12.00   ☐

2011 The Genius of Gerry Anderson (11th January)

Full of images, photos and illustrations, this pack contains an interview with Gerry Anderson and details the process of Supermarionation, his own form of puppet animation. Enclosed is also a limited edition Thunderbirds comic book, fully illustrated by Gerry Embleton. **Note:** An additional minisheet of stamps is included in the back of the pack.

Limited edition comic book

PP424   2011 The Genius of Gerry Anderson
         (printed no.450)   19.00   ☐

2011 Classic Locomotives of England (1st February)

Containing archive photos throughout, this pack tells the story behind each of the classic locomotives featured on the enclosed stamps.

PP425   2011 Classic Locomotives of England
         (printed no.451)   7.00   ☐

2011 Musicals (24th February)

Celebrating the long and rich history of music in the British theatre, this pack focusses on the writers, actors and number of shows of each of the musicals featured on the enclosed stamps.

PP426   2011 Musicals (printed no.452)   11.00   ☐

2011 Magical Realms (8th March)

Starting with most famous literary magician, Merlin, this illustrated pack discusses the wizards and witches of our great mythical stories and the magical realms they inhabit.

PP427   2011 Magical Realms (printed no.453)   10.00   ☐

2011 World Wildlife Fund (22nd March)

As the WWF celebrated its 50th Anniversary, the 10 animals featured in this pack were considered 'vulnerable', 'endangered' or 'critically endangered'. Contains photos, facts and figures about each animal and the WWF's efforts to save them. **Note:** An additional minisheet of stamps is included in the back of the pack.

PP428   2011 World Wildlife Fund (printed no.454)   14.00   ☐

2011 Royal Shakespeare Company (12th April)

Commemorating the 50th Anniversary of the RSC, this pack is full of information about the rich variety of their productions. Contains two montages of images from front of stage and behind the scenes, along with a timeline of the Company events. **Note:** An additional minisheet of stamps is included in the back of the pack.

PP429   2011 Royal Shakespeare Company
(printed no.455)   13.50   ☐

2011 The Royal Wedding (21st April)

To commemorate the marriage of HRH Prince William and Catherine Middleton, this pack tells the story of their meeting at University and subsequent relationship prior to engagement. Written in English and Welsh.

PP430   2011 The Royal Wedding (printed no.M20)   12.00   ☐

2011 Morris and Co. (5th May)

Illustrated throughout with examples of his unmistakable designs, this pack tells of William Morris's life and the great success of his business partnerships.

PP431   2011 Morris and Co. (printed no.456)   10.00   ☐

2011 Thomas the Tank Engine (14th June)

In tribute to his father Reverend Wilbert V Awdry, creator of The Railway Series, Christopher Awdry tells the story behind Thomas the Tank Engine and his friends. Contains images of original sketches, photos of the author and TV stills. **Note:** An additional minisheet of stamps is included in the back of the pack.

PP432   2011 Thomas the Tank Engine
(printed no.457)   14.00   ☐

2011 Olympic & Paralympic Games (27th July)

This pack contains facts and figures about the 10 sports featured on the enclosed stamps and some of the disciplines within them, along with illustrations representing each one.

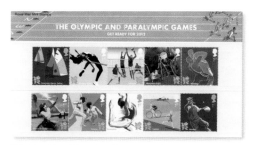

PP433   2011 Olympic & Paralympic Games
(printed no.458)   11.00   ☐

2011 The Crown Jewels (23rd August)

The history, the beauty and the function of the British Crown Jewels are detailed and illustrated in this pack along with information about the Coronation procession and ceremony, which is the oldest of any in Europe.

PP434   2011 The Crown Jewels (printed no.459)   11.00   ☐

2011 Aerial Post (9th September)

Commemorating the Centenary of Gustav Hamel's first flight from Hendon to Windsor, this pack looks at the plans, preparations and aviators behind the first aerial post service. Contains photos, images of memorabilia and a log of the mails.

PP435   2011 Aerial Post (printed no.460)   7.00   ☐

2011 The House of Hanover (15th September)

Under the Hanoverians, politics shifted from court to Parliament. This pack tells of big political changes and expansion of the British empire. Contains images of paintings from the period. **Note:** An additional minisheet of stamps is included in the back of the pack.

PP436   2011 The House of Hanover
(printed no.461)   13.00   ☐

2011 UK A-Z Part 1 (13th October)

An alphabetical journey through some of the finest creations in the UK, this pack contains images and information about the 12 icons featured on the enclosed stamps.

PP437   2011 UK A-Z Part 1 (printed no.462)   12.00   ☐

2011 Christmas (8th November)

This pack focusses on the history of the King James Bible and of Bible translation. It is designed on the same page grid, and at actual size, as a page from the original.

PP438   2011 Christmas (printed no.463)   11.00   ☐

2012 Roald Dahl (10th January)

Written by Donald Sturrock and illustrated by Quentin Blake, this pack gives a brief synopsis of Roald Dahl's life and of his working relationship with Quentin Blake. **Note:** An additional minisheet of stamps is included in the back of the pack.

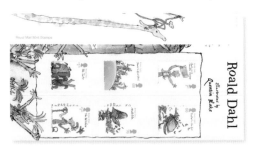

PP439   2012 Roald Dahl (printed no.465)   14.00   ☐

2012 The House of Windsor (2nd February)

The last in the series of 'Kings and Queens', this pack contains information and photos of some of the ground-breaking changes that have occurred during the reigns of the House of Windsor. **Note:** An additional minisheet of stamps is included in the back of the pack.

PP440   2012 The House of Windsor
(printed no.466)   12.00   ☐

2012 Britons of Distinction (23rd February)

Containing photos and illustrations for each, this pack celebrates the work of 10 Britons of distinction, including the brilliant mathematician Alan Turing.

PP441   2012 Britons of Distinction (printed no.467)   8.00   ☐

2012 Classic Locomotives of Scotland
(8th March)

Containing photos, illustrations and images throughout, this pack gives a wealth of information about Scotland's railway history, eminent engineers and preservation.

PP442   2012 Classic Locomotives of Scotland
(printed no.468)   6.50   ☐

2012 Comics (20th March)

Celebrating 75 years of British comics, this colourful pack features illustrations, statistics and information about 10 of the most popular titles. Contains a seperate 12-page reproduction of comic strips from the first ever 'Dandy'.

Inside the pack is a reproduction comic strip

PP443   2012 Comics (printed no.469)   11.00   ☐

2012 UK A-Z Part 2 (10th April)

An alphabetical journey that reflects the breadth and depth of the UK's heritage, this pack contains images and information about the fourteen landmarks featured on the enclosed stamps.

PP444   2012 UK A-Z Part 2 (printed no.470)   14.00   ☐

2012 Great British Fashion (15th May)

Highlighting 10 influential British designers, this pack provides an overview of British fashion since 1945 and contains photos and images that represent each major period of change.

PP445   2012 Great British Fashion (printed no.471)   12.00   ☐

2012 The Diamond Jubilee (31st May)

Commemorating 60 years of service, and with photos throughout, this pack looks at the role of Her Majesty The Queen as monarch and some of her ceremonial duties.

PP446   2012 The Diamond Jubilee (printed no.472)   20.00   ☐

2012 Charles Dickens (9th June)

Marking the Bicentenary of the birth of Charles Dickens, this pack tells of the life and legacy of the greatest novelist of his generation. Contains illustrations of original book covers and a map showing fifteen locations in London closely associated with Dickens' life. **Note:** An additional minisheet of stamps is included in the back of the pack.

PP447   2012 Charles Dickens (printed no.473)   14.50   ☐

2012 Welcome to the Olympic Games (27th July)

Celebrating the 30th Olympiad, held in London, this pack contains an impressive collection of statistics, facts and figures relating to the greatest show on Earth and its host city.

PP448   2012 Welcome to the Olympic Games
(printed no.474)   20.00   ☐

2012 Welcome to the Paralympic Games (29th August)

This pack contains a brief history of the Paralympic Games and two map-style illustrations that separately indicate Olympic Park venues and Paralympic venues alongside famous London landmarks.

PP449   2012 Welcome to the Paralympic Games
(printed no.475)   10.00   ☐

2012 Memories of London 2012 (27th September)

Commemorating the London 2012 Games, this pack contains listings of all 63 gold medal winners from Team GB and Paralympics GB, along with quotations and photos of some of the athletes.

PP450   2012 Memories of London 2012
(printed no.476)   13.00   ☐

2012 Space Science (16th October)

This fully illustrated pack looks at the planets and moons of the solar system and some of the spacecraft sent on missions to discover more about them. Contains details of some recent discoveries.

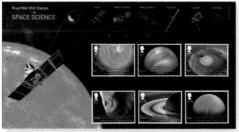

PP451   2012 Space Science (printed no.477)   10.00   ☐

2012 Christmas (6th November)

This pack contains a short, specially written Christmas story which is fully illustrated by Axel Scheffler. The story relates to the enclosed stamps.

PP452   2012 Christmas (printed no.478)   16.00   ☐

2013 London Underground (8th January)

Marking the 150th Anniversary of the opening of the first urban underground service in the world, this pack gives the history of the London Underground. Contains illustrations, images and photos from c. 1870 to 2012. **Note:** An additional minisheet of stamps is included in the back of the pack.

PP453   2013 London Underground
(printed no.480)   14.00   ☐

2013 Jane Austen (21st February)

To commemorate the 200th Anniversary of the publication of Pride and Prejudice, this pack studies the book that inspired generations and takes a look at the genius behind it. Contains illustrations, excerpts and quotations.

PP454   2013 Jane Austen (printed no.481)   10.00   ☐

2013 Doctor Who (26th March)

Celebrating 50 years of Doctor Who, this pack features the 10 Doctors and their assistants, and describes each man's idiosyncrasies. Contains photos of all the Doctors and some of his arch rivals. **Note:** An additional minisheet of stamps is included in the back of the pack.

PP455   2013 Doctor Who (printed no.482)   15.00   ☐

2013 Great Britons (16th April)

In celebration of the lives of the 10 distinguished individuals featured on the enclosed stamps, this pack gives a brief insight into the life and work of each. Contains accompanying images, movie stills and photos.

PP456   2013 Great Britons (printed no.483)   10.00   ☐

2013 Football Heroes (9th May)

Containing photos and images of memorabilia, this pack celebrates the careers of the eleven football 'heroes' featured on the enclosed stamps. There is also a set of career statistics for each player.

PP457   2013 Football Heroes (printed no.484)   11.00 ☐

2013 Her Majesty The Queen (30th May)

To mark the 60th Anniversary of The Queen's coronation, Royal Mail commissioned a portrait of her. This pack celebrates six decades of painted royal portraiture by describing the new commission along with five others. Contains images of the paintings and details of the artists.

PP458   2013 Her Majesty The Queen
(printed no.485)   10.00 ☐

2013 Classic Locomotives of Northern Ireland

(18th June)
Containing archive photos throughout, this pack tells the story behind each of the classic locomotives featured on the enclosed stamps, along with details of Northern Ireland's railway system.

PP459   2013 Classic Locomotives of Northern Ireland
(printed no.486)   7.00 ☐

2013 Butterflies (11th July)

This pack contains information about the 10 butterfly species featured on the enclosed stamps, including a fully illustrated life cycle and the preferred habitat of each one.

PP460   2013 Butterflies (printed no.487)   10.00 ☐

2013 Andy Murray (6th August)

Having finally become a Wimbledon Champion, Andy Murray's path to success is noted in this pack along with photos and details of his historic victory.

PP461   2013 Andy Murray (printed no.M21)   7.00 ☐

2013 British Auto Legends (13th August)

Launched in 1961, the E-Type Jaguar changed the face of car design. Along with five other legends of the British motor industry, this pack features archive photos, illustrations and technical specifications. **Note:** An additional minisheet of stamps is included in the back of the pack.

PP462   2013 British Auto Legends (printed no.488) 12.50 ☐

2013 Merchant Navy (19th September)

The crucial role of the Merchant Navy is highlighted in this pack and illustrated with wartime photos. It also looks at the history of the six vessels featured on the enclosed stamps, with accompanying images. **Note:** An additional minisheet of stamps is included in the back of the pack.

PP463   2013 Merchant Navy (printed no.489)   12.50   ☐

2013 Dinosaurs (10th October)

This fascinating pack studies the earliest discoveries of dinosaurs, which occurred in England during the early 1800s. Focussing on the 10 species featured on the enclosed stamps, the pack contains illustrations, facts and figures, a timeline and details of the UK fossil sites.

PP464   2013 Dinosaurs (printed no.490)   10.00   ☐

2013 Children's Christmas (5th November)

Celebrating the joy of Christmas, this pack features the 24 shortlisted entries from Royal Mail's nationwide children's competition to design 1st Class and 2nd Class Christmas stamps.

PP465   2013 Children's Christmas (printed no.M22)   3.00   ☐

2013 Christmas (5th November)

The Madonna and Child theme is common to many world religions and this pack studies the development and range of artistic representations over the past 600 years, with a particular focus on Coptic Art. Contains images of beautiful artworks throughout.

PP466   2013 Christmas (printed no.491)   12.00   ☐

2014 Classic Children's TV (7th January)

In this lavishly illustrated pack, television writer Graham Kibble-White discusses the golden age of children's TV from the 1950s to the present day, with a synopsis of each series.

PP467   2014 Classic Children's TV (printed no.493)   12.00   ☐

2014 Working Horses (4th February)

Looking at the history of horse power, this pack studies the many ways that the working horse has contributed to human life and labour, and how they continue to be used today. Contains photos and illustrations throughout.

PP468   2014 Working Horses (printed no.494)   9.50   ☐

2014 Classic Locomotives of Wales (20th February)

Containing archive photos throughout, this pack tells the story behind each of the classic locomotives featured on the enclosed stamps, along with details of the Welsh railway system. Written in English and Welsh.

| PP469 | 2014 Classic Locomotives of Wales (printed no.495) | 6.50 | ☐ |

2014 Remarkable Lives (25th March)

This fully illustrated and highly informative pack covers key moments in the lives of the 10 individuals shown on the enclosed stamps and provides a comprehensive overview of each person's achievements.

| PP470 | 2014 Remarkable Lives (printed no.496) | 8.00 | ☐ |

Definitive Packs

This section includes all packs containing definitive stamps i.e 'high' and 'low' value packs, and 'country' packs where the enclosed stamps are specific to either England, Scotland, Wales or Northern Ireland. Typically, Definitive Packs are issued in line with a change to postage rates.

1969 Machin 2/6 to £1 (5th March)

The first pack of high value Machin stamps, it details the change of design from Wilding's portrait of The Queen to Machin's sculpted image. Contains four stamps from 2/6 to £1.

1969 Machin ½d to 1/9 (5th March)

This pack details the change of stamp design from Wilding's portrait of The Queen to Machin's sculpted image. A total of 16 Machin stamps were issued between 1967 and 1969. This is the first pack containing stamps from ½d to 1/9.

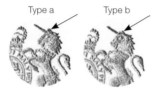

Type a   Type b

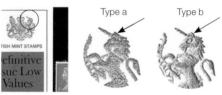

Type a   Type b

PPD1 g

PPD2 g

The definitive issue: high values
確定発行の高額切手

PPD2	1969 Machin ½d to 1/9		9.00	☐
a	One tuft on Unicorn's head	9.00	☐	
b	Two tufts on Unicorn's head	9.00	☐	
g	German language pack	140.00	☐	

PPD1	1969 Machin 2/6 to £1		15.00	☐
a	One tuft on Unicorn's head	15.00	☐	
b	Two tufts on Unicorn's head	35.00	☐	
g	German language pack	80.00	☐	
j	Japanese insert card	200.00	☐	

1970 Machin 10p - 50p (17th June)

The first pack of decimal Machin stamps, it details every high value stamp from 1867 with an image of each one. Contains three stamps from 10p to 50p.

PPD3	1970 Machin 10p - 50p (printed no.18)	12.00	☐
g	German insert card [PL(P)2096A]	9.00	☐
j	Japanese insert card [PL(P)2096B]	9.00	☐

1970 Scotland (9th December)

One of the first Country packs of definitives, containing some information on Scotland's geography and culture. Contains eight stamps from 3d to 1/6. (Qty. sold 31,476)

| PPD4 | 1970 Scotland (printed no.23) | 7.00 | ☐ |

1970 Wales and Monmouthshire (9th December)

One of the first Country packs, containing some information on Wales and Monmouthshire's landscape and culture. Contains six stamps from 3d to 1/6. (Qty. sold 32,964)

PPD5   1970 Wales and Monmouthshire (printed no.24) 4.00 ☐

1970 Northern Ireland (9th December)

A Country pack of definitives, containing some information on Northern Ireland's commerce and industry. Contains seven stamps from 3d to 1/6. (Qty. sold 28,944)

| PPD6 | 1970 Northern Ireland (printed no.25) | 4.00 | ☐ |

1971 Machin ½ to 9p (15th February)

The first pack of low value decimal Machin stamps, it details every low value stamp from 1840, with an image of each. Contains 12 stamps from ½ to 9p. These were also issued in the 'Scandinavia' pack - see Special Edition section.

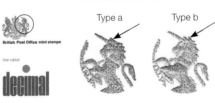

Type a   Type b

PPD7	1971 Machin ½ to 9p (printed no.26)	6.00	☐
a	One tuft on Unicorn's head	6.00	☐
b	Two tufts on Unicorn's head	8.00	☐
g	German insert card [PL(P)2129A]	7.50	☐
j	Japanese insert card [PL(P)2129B]	7.50	☐

1971 Scotland (7th July)

This Country pack of definitives contains some information on Scotland's great cities and traditions. Contains four stamps from 2½p to 7½p.

Type a   Type b

PPD8	1971 Scotland (printed no.27)	3.50	☐
a	No spur on Lion's hind leg	3.50	☐
b	Spur on Lion's hind leg	4.50	☐
g	German insert card	110.00	☐

1971 Wales (7th July)

This Country pack of definitives contains some information on the diversity of Wales. Written in English and Welsh. Contains four stamps from 2½p to 7½p.

PPD9	1971 Wales (printed no.28)	3.50	☐
g	German insert card	110.00	☐

1971 Northern Ireland (7th July)

This Country pack of definitives contains some information on the six counties of Northern Ireland. Contains four stamps from 2½p to 7½p.

PPD10	1971 Northern Ireland (printed no.29)	3.50	☐
g	German insert card	110.00	☐

1971 Isle of Man (7th July)

This Country pack of definitives contains some information on the island's history, traditions and varied landscapes. Contains four stamps from 2½p to 7½p.

PPD11	1971 Isle of Man (printed no.30)	2.50	☐
g	German insert card	110.00	☐

1971 Machin ½ to 10p (25th November)

This pack details every low value stamp from 1840, with an image of each. Contains 16 stamps from ½ to 10p. **Note:** stamp configurations vary widely in line with the disclaimer inside the pack "Any future alterations will be included in this pack as they occur". Later issues included the 6½p and 7p stamps, and many other configurations have been seen.

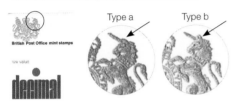

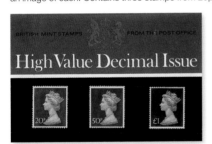

| | Type a | Type b |
| | | |

PPD12	1971 Machin ½ to 10p (printed no.37)	24.00	☐
	a No bump on Unicorn's head	24.00	☐
	b Bump on Unicorn's head	24.00	☐

1971 Machin 20p - £1 (25th November)

This pack details every high value stamp issued since 1867, with an image of each. Contains three stamps from 20p to £1.

| PPD13 | 1971 Machin 20p - £1 (printed no.38) | 16.00 | ☐ |

1974 Northern Ireland (29th May)

This Country pack of definitives contains some information on Northern Ireland's six counties. Contains four stamps from 3p to 8p. Later issues also included 4½p stamp.

| PPD14 | 1974 Northern Ireland (printed no.61) | 2.50 | ☐ |

1974 Scotland (29th May)

This Country pack of definitives contains some information on the design of the stamps. Contains four stamps from 3p to 8p. Later issues also included 4½p stamp.

| PPD15 | 1974 Scotland (printed no.62) | 2.50 | ☐ |

1974 Wales (29th May)

This Country pack of definitives contains some information on the industry and culture of Wales. Written in English and Welsh. Contains four stamps from 3p to 8p. Later issues also included 4½p stamp.

| PPD16 | 1974 Wales (printed no.63) | 2.50 | ☐ |

1976 Northern Ireland (20th October)

This Country pack of definitives contains some information on Northern Ireland's landscapes and legends. Contains four stamps from 6½p to 11p.

PPD17   1976 Northern Ireland (printed no.84)   2.00   ☐

1976 Scotland (20th October)

This Country pack of definitives contains some information on Scotland's flag, the Saltire and the heraldic Lion. Contains four stamps from 6½p to 11p.

PPD18   1976 Scotland (printed no.85)   2.00   ☐

1976 Wales (20th October)

This Country pack of definitives contains some information on the Royal Badge of Wales and its Red Dragon. Written in English and Welsh. Contains four stamps from 6½p to 11p.

PPD19   1976 Wales (printed no.86)   2.00   ☐

1977 Machin ½ to 50p (2nd February)

Low value definitive stamps issued in 1977. Inside tells of Machin's detailed sculpture of the Queen and how it was incorporated onto the stamps. Contains 19 stamps from ½p to 50p.

PPD20   1977 Machin ½ to 50p (printed no.90)   5.00   ☐

1977 Machin £1 to £5 (2nd February)

This pack details every high value stamp issued since 1867, with an image of each. Contains three stamps from £1 to £5.

PPD21   1977 Machin £1 to £5 (printed no.91)   18.00   ☐

1981 Machin 2½p to 75p (28th October)

This pack is similar to pack PPD20, but with a small sticker saying "129a", covering the original Post Office pack number of 127a. Contains 18 stamps from 2½p to 75p.

PPD22   1981 Machin 2½p to 75p (printed no.129a)   16.00   ☐

1981 Scotland (28th October)

This Country pack of definitives contains some information on Scotland's flag, the Saltire and the heraldic Lion. Contains six stamps from 10½p to 22p.

PPD23   1976 Scotland (printed no.129b)   7.50   ☐

1981 Wales (28th October)

This Country pack of definitives contains some information on the Royal Badge of Wales and its Red Dragon. Written in English and Welsh. Contains six stamps from 10½p to 22p.

PPD24   1976 Wales (printed no.129c)   7.50   ☐

1981 Northern Ireland (28th October)

This Country pack of definitives contains some information on Northern Ireland's landscapes and legends. Contains six stamps from 10½p to 22p.

PPD25   1976 Northern Ireland (printed no.129d)   7.50   ☐

1983 Machin ½ to 75p (3rd August)

This is the first low value definitives pack printed in medium format size. It discusses Machin's detailed sculpture of The Queen and how it was incorporated onto the stamps. Contains 20 stamps from ½ to 75p.

PPD26   1983 Machin ½ to 75p (printed no.1)   30.00   ☐

1983 Scotland (3rd August)

This Country pack tells the history of the heraldic Lion of Scotland, thought to have been introduced during the reign of William the Lion (1165-1214). Contains six stamps from 10p to 28p.

PPD27   1983 Scotland (printed no.2)   14.00   ☐

1983 Wales (3rd August)

This Country pack tells of the symbol of the Dragon of Wales and its inclusion on the Royal Badge of Wales. Written in English and Welsh. Contains six stamps from 10p to 28p.

PPD28   1983 Wales (printed no.3)   14.00   ☐

1983 Northern Ireland (3rd August)

This Country pack tells of The Red Right Hand of Ulster, which originated from Hugh O'Neill, King of Ulster (1347-1364). Contains six stamps from 10p to 28p.

PPD29   1983 Northern Ireland (printed no.4)   14.00   ☐

1984 Machin ½ to 75p (23rd October)

This pack contains a set of low value definitives. Inside tells of Machin's detailed sculpture of The Queen and how it was incorporated onto the stamps. Contains 20 stamps from ½ to 75p.

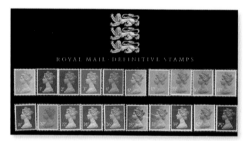

PPD30   1984 Machin ½ to 75p (printed no.5)   18.00   ☐

1984 Scotland (23rd October)

This Country pack tells the history of the heraldic Lion of Scotland, thought to have been introduced during the reign of William the Lion (1165-1214). Contains eight stamps from 10p to 31p.

PPD31   1984 Scotland (printed no.6)   11.00   ☐

1984 Wales (23rd October)

This Country pack tells of the symbol of the Dragon of Wales and its inclusion on the Royal Badge of Wales. Written in English and Welsh. Contains eight stamps from 10p to 31p.

PPD32   1984 Wales (printed no.7)   11.00   ☐

1984 Northern Ireland (23rd October)

This Country pack tells of The Red Right Hand of Ulster, which originated from Hugh O'Neill, King of Ulster (1347-1364). Contains eight stamps from 10p to 31p.

PPD33   1984 Northern Ireland (printed no.8)   11.00   ☐

1987 Machin 1p to 75p (3rd March)

This pack contains a set of low value definitives. Inside tells of Machin's detailed sculpture of The Queen and how it was incorporated onto the stamps. Contains 20 stamps from 1p to 75p.

PPD34   1987 Machin 1p to 75p (printed no.9)   30.00   ☐

1987 Scotland (3rd March)

This Country pack tells the history of the heraldic Lion of Scotland, thought to have been introduced during the reign of William the Lion (1165-1214). Contains eight stamps from 12p to 31p.

| PPD35 | 1987 Scotland (printed no.10) | 12.00 | ☐ |

1987 Wales (3rd March)

This Country pack tells of the symbol of the Dragon of Wales and its inclusion on the Royal Badge of Wales. Written in English and Welsh. Contains eight stamps from 12p to 31p.

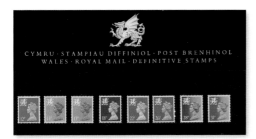

| PPD36 | 1987 Wales (printed no.11) | 12.00 | ☐ |

1987 Northern Ireland (3rd March)

This Country pack tells of The Red Right Hand of Ulster, which originated from Hugh O'Neill, King of Ulster (1347-1364). It was the last of the single 'country' packs to be produced until 1997. Contains eight stamps from 12p to 31p.

| PPD37 | 1987 Northern Ireland (printed no.12) | 12.00 | ☐ |

1987 Machin £1 to £5 (3rd March)

This pack contains a set of high value definitives. Inside tells of Machin's detailed sculpture of The Queen and how it was incorporated onto the stamps. Contains three stamps from £1 to £5.

| PPD38 | 1987 Machin £1 to £5 (printed no.13) | 160.00 | ☐ |

1987 Machin £1.60 (15th September)

This pack contains one high value definitive. Inside tells of Machin's detailed sculpture of The Queen and how it was incorporated onto the stamp. Contains one stamp at £1.60.

| PPD39 | 1987 Machin £1.60 (printed no.14) | 16.00 | ☐ |

1988 Machin 14p to 35p (23rd August)

This pack contains a set of low value definitives. Inside tells of Machin's detailed sculpture of The Queen and how it was incorporated onto the stamps. Contains eight stamps from 14p to 35p.

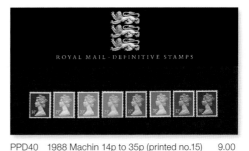

| PPD40 | 1988 Machin 14p to 35p (printed no.15) | 9.00 | ☐ |

1988 Castles £1 to £5 (18th October)

This pack is the first in the series of 'Castles'. Inside is a brief history of each castle represented; Carrickfergus, Caernarfon, Edinburgh and Windsor. Contains four stamps from £1 to £5, each of which was designed by HRH The Duke of York.

PPD41   1988 Castles £1 to £5 (printed no.18)   17.50   ☐
Also exists as an Error - Gold image missing

1988 Three Regions (8th November)

This pack is the first to include stamps of Scotland, Wales and Northern Ireland. Inside is a brief history of the symbols illustrated on the cover. Contains three sets of four stamps from 14p to 32p.

PPD42   1988 Three Regions (printed no.17)   9.00   ☐

1989 Machin 15p to 37p (26th September)

This pack contains a set of low value definitives. Inside tells of Machin's detailed sculpture of The Queen and how it was incorporated onto the stamps. Contains seven stamps from 15p to 37p.

PPD43   1989 Machin 15p to 37p (printed no.19)   6.00   ☐

1989 Three Regions (28th November)

This pack contains stamps of Scotland, Wales and Northern Ireland. Inside is a brief history of the symbols illustrated on the cover. Contains three sets of four stamps from 15p to 34p.

PPD44   1988 Three Regions (printed no.20)   9.00   ☐

1990 Penny Black Anniversary (10th January)

This pack commemorates the 150th Anniversary of the Penny Black and tells how Rowland Hill devised our postage system. Contains five stamps from 15p to 37p.

PPD45   1990 Penny Black Anniversary
(printed no.21)   7.00   ☐

1990 Machin 10p to 33p (4th September)

This pack contains a set of low value definitives. Inside tells of Machin's detailed sculpture of The Queen and how it was incorporated onto the stamps. Contains seven stamps from 10p to 33p.

PPD46   1990 Machin 10p to 33p (printed no.22)   7.00   ☐

1990 Three Regions (4th December)

This pack contains stamps of Scotland, Wales and Northern Ireland. Inside is a brief history of the symbols illustrated on the cover. Contains three sets of four stamps from 17p to 37p.

| PPD47 | 1990 Three Regions (printed no.23) | 9.00 | □ |

1991 Three Regions (3rd December)

This pack contains stamps of Scotland, Wales and Northern Ireland. Inside is a brief history of the symbols illustrated on the cover. Contains three sets of four stamps from 18p to 39p.

| PPD50 | 1991 Three Regions (printed no.26) | 9.00 | □ |

1991 Machin 1p to 75p (14th May)

This pack contains a set of low value definitives. Inside tells of Machin's detailed sculpture of The Queen and how it was incorporated onto the stamps. Contains 18 stamps from 1p to 75p.

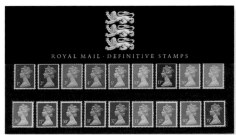

| PPD48 | 1991 Machin 1p to 75p (printed no.24) | 25.00 | □ |

1992 Castles £1 to £5 (24th March)

The second pack in the series of 'Castles'. Inside is a brief history of each castle represented; Carrickfergus, Caernarfon, Edinburgh and Windsor. Contains four stamps from £1 to £5, each of which was designed by HRH The Duke of York.

| PPD51 | 1992 Castles £1 to £5 (printed no.27) | 17.50 | □ |

1991 Machin 6p to 39p (10th September)

This pack contains a set of low value definitives. Inside tells of Machin's detailed sculpture of The Queen and how it was incorporated onto the stamps. Contains seven stamps from 6p to 39p.

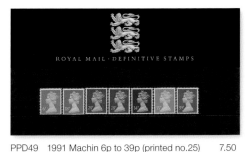

| PPD49 | 1991 Machin 6p to 39p (printed no.25) | 7.50 | □ |

1993 Britannia £10 (2nd March)

This highly decorative and illustrated pack gives a history of the popular and heroic figure Britannia, from first use on Roman coinage over 1,800 years ago. Contains one stamp of £10 value.

| PPD52 | 1993 Britannia £10 (printed no.28) | 22.00 | □ |

1993 Machin 1st Booklet (19th October)

After years of research and development, this pack heralds the Royal Mail's introduction of self-adhesive stamps, which offered users a new level of convenience. Contains a book of 20 1st Class, self-adhesive, stamps.

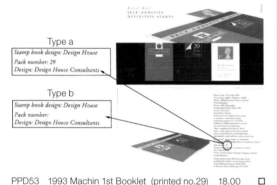

Type a

Stamp book design: Design House
Pack number: 29
Design: Design House Consultants

Type b

Stamp book design: Design House
Pack number:
Design: Design House Consultants

PPD53	1993 Machin 1st Booklet (printed no.29)	18.00	□
	a Pack number included	18.00	□
	b Pack number missing	18.00	□

1993 Machin 19p to 41p (26th October)

This pack contains a set of low value definitives. Inside tells of Machin's detailed sculpture of The Queen and how it was incorporated onto the stamps. Contains six stamps from 19p to 41p.

| PPD54 | 1993 Machin 19p to 41p (printed no.30) | 5.00 | □ |

1993 Three Regions (7th December)

This pack contains stamps of Scotland, Wales and Northern Ireland. Inside is a brief history of the symbols illustrated on the cover. Contains three sets of four stamps from 19p to 41p.

| PPD55 | 1993 Three Regions (printed no.31) | 9.00 | □ |

1995 Castle £3 (22nd August)

The third pack in the series of 'Castles'. Inside is a brief history of each castle represented on the two previous packs; Carrickfergus, Caernarfon, Edinburgh and Windsor. Contains one stamp of £3 value, which was designed by HRH The Duke of York.

| PPD56 | 1995 Castle £3 (printed no.33) | 14.00 | □ |

1995 Machin 1p to £1 (21st November)

This pack contains a set of low value definitives. Inside tells of Machin's detailed sculpture of The Queen and how it was incorporated onto the stamps. Contains 18 stamps from 1p to £1.

| PPD57 | 1995 Machin 1p to £1 (printed no.34) | 27.50 | □ |

1996 Machin 20p to 63p (25th June)

This pack contains a set of low value definitives. Inside tells of Machin's detailed sculpture of The Queen and how it was incorporated onto the stamps. Contains seven stamps from 20p to 63p.

PPD58   1996 Machin 20p to 63p (printed no.35)   7.50   ☐

1996 Three Regions (23rd July)

This pack contains stamps of Scotland, Wales and Northern Ireland. Inside is a brief history of the symbols illustrated on the cover. Contains three sets of four stamps from 20p to 63p.

PPD59   1996 Three Regions (printed no.36)   9.00   ☐

1997 Machin 2nd & 1st (18th March)

This is the second pack to contain self-adhesive stamps. Inside tells of the 'Machin definitive' design and the return to the photogravure method of printing. Contains a 2nd Class stamp and a 1st Class stamp.

PPD60   1997 Machin 2nd & 1st (printed no.37)   5.50   ☐

1997 Machin 26p & 1st (21st April)

Inside this pack tells of Machin's detailed sculpture of The Queen and how it was incorporated onto postage stamps, including various methods of printing. Contains a 26p stamp and a 1st Class stamp.

PPD61   1997 Machin 26p & 1st (printed no.38)   5.50   ☐

1997 Wales (1st July)

This Country pack, the first to be issued since the 1987 Northern Ireland pack, tells of the symbol of the Dragon of Wales and its inclusion on the Royal Badge of Wales. Written in English and Welsh. Contains four stamps from 20p to 63p, although the 'p' after the numerals was omitted.

PPD62   1997 Wales (printed no.39)   9.00   ☐

1997 Castles £1.50 to £5 (29th July)

The fourth pack in the series of 'Castles', this was the last one produced for eight years. Inside is a brief history of each castle represented; Caernarfon, Edinburgh, Carrickfergus and Windsor. Contains four stamps from £1.50 to £5, each of which was designed by HRH The Duke of York.

PPD63   1997 Castles £1.50 to £5 (printed no.40)   85.00   ☐

1998 Machin 1p to £1, 2nd & 1st (20th October)

This pack contains a set of low value definitives. Inside tells of Machin's detailed sculpture of The Queen and how it was incorporated onto the stamps. Contains 18 stamps from 1p to £1, plus 2nd and 1st Class.

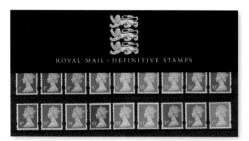

PPD64	1998 Machin 1p to £1, 2nd & 1st (printed no.41)	13.00	☐

1998 Three Regions (20th October)

This pack contains stamps of Scotland, Wales and Northern Ireland. Inside is a brief history of the symbols illustrated on the cover. Contains three sets of four stamps from 20p to 63p. The 'p' after the numerals was omitted from the Welsh stamps.

PPD65	1998 Three Regions (printed no.42)	20.00	☐

1999 Machin £1.50 to £5 (9th March)

This pack contains a set of high value definitives. Inside tells of Machin's detailed sculpture of The Queen and how it was incorporated onto the stamps. Contains four stamps from £1.50 to £5.

PPD66	1999 Machin £1.50 to £5 (printed no.43)	32.00	☐

1999 Machin 7p to 64p (20th April)

This pack contains a set of low value definitives. Inside tells of Machin's detailed sculpture of The Queen and how it was incorporated onto the stamps. Contains five stamps from 7p to 64p.

PPD67	1999 Machin 7p to 64p (printed no.44)	9.00	☐

1999 Scotland (8th June)

This Country pack commemorates Scotland's first elected Parliament in almost 300 years with the introduction of a new design. It includes some attractive photography and information on Scotland's geology. Contains four stamps from 2nd Class to 64p.

PPD68	1999 Scotland (printed no.45)	9.50	☐

1999 Wales (8th June)

This Country pack commemorates the creation of the Welsh National Assembly with the introduction of a new design and some attractive photography. Written in English and Welsh. Contains four stamps from 2nd Class to 64p.

PPD69	1999 Wales (printed no.46)	9.50	☐

1999 Northern Ireland (8th June)

This Country pack tells of The Red Right Hand of Ulster, which originated from Hugh O'Neill, King of Ulster (1347-1364). Contains four stamps from 19p to 64p.

| PPD70 | 1999 Northern Ireland (printed no.47) | 5.40 | ☐ |

2000 Machin 1st (6th January)

This pack tells of Machin's detailed sculpture of The Queen and how it was incorporated onto the stamps. Contains one 1st Class stamp.

| PPD71 | 2000 Machin 1st (printed no.48) | 5.00 | ☐ |

2000 Machin 8p to 65p (25th April)

This pack contains a set of low value definitives. Inside tells of Machin's detailed sculpture of The Queen and how it was incorporated onto the stamps. Contains six stamps from 8p to 65p.

| PPD72 | 2000 Machin 8p to 65p (printed no.49) | 9.00 | ☐ |

2000 Scotland (25th April)

This Country pack commemorates Scotland's first elected Parliament in almost 300 years. It includes some attractive photography and information on Scotland's geology. Contains one 65p stamp.

| PPD73 | 2000 Scotland (printed no.50) | 8.00 | ☐ |

2000 Wales (25th April)

This Country pack commemorates the creation of the Welsh National Assembly with some attractive photography. Written in English and Welsh. Contains one 65p stamp.

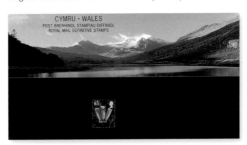

| PPD74 | 2000 Wales (printed no.51) | 8.00 | ☐ |

2000 Northern Ireland (25th April)

This Country pack tells of The Red Right Hand of Ulster, which originated from Hugh O'Neill, King of Ulster (1347-1364). Contains three stamps from 1st Class to 65p.

| PPD75 | 2000 Northern Ireland (printed no.52) | 10.00 | ☐ |

2001 Northern Ireland (6th March)

This Country pack heralds a new era for Northern Ireland with the introduction of a new design. It includes some attractive photography and information on Northern Ireland's rural landscape. Contains four stamps from 2nd Class to 65p.

| PPD76 | 2001 Northern Ireland (printed no.53) | 7.00 | ☐ |

2001 England (23rd April)

This was the first Country pack specific to England. It celebrates the diversity of England's landscape, including some attractive photography, and discusses the influence of English flora. Contains four stamps from 2nd Class to 65p.

| PPD77 | 2001 England (printed no.54) | 7.00 | ☐ |

2002 Machin £1.50 to £5 (12th March)

This pack contains a set of high value definitives. It is the first pack to bear the Royal emblem of the St. Edward's crown. Inside tells of Machin's detailed sculpture of the Queen and how it was incorporated onto the stamps. Contains four stamps from £1.50 to £5.

| PPD78 | 2002 Machin £1.50 to £5 (printed no.43a) | 32.00 | ☐ |

2002 Scotland (12th March)

This Country pack commemorates Scotland's first elected Parliament in almost 300 years. It includes some attractive photography and information on Scotland's geology. Contains four stamps from 2nd Class to 65p.

| PPD79 | 2002 Scotland (printed no.55) | 13.00 | ☐ |

2002 Wales (12th March)

This Country pack commemorates the creation of the Welsh National Assembly with some attractive photography. Written in English and Welsh. Contains four stamps from 2nd Class to 65p.

| PPD80 | 2002 Wales (printed no.56) | 13.00 | ☐ |

2002 Machin 1p to £1, 2nd & 1st (12th March)

This pack contains a set of low value definitives. Inside tells of Machin's detailed sculpture of the Queen and how it was incorporated onto the stamps. Contains 17 stamps from 1p to £1, 2nd Class and 1st Class.

| PPD81 | 2002 Machin 1p to £1, 2nd & 1st (printed no.57) | 14.00 | ☐ |

2002 Machin 37p to 68p (4th July)

This pack contains a set of low value definitives. Inside tells of Machin's detailed sculpture of the Queen and how it was incorporated onto the stamps. Contains four stamps from 37p to 68p.

PPD82   2002 Machin 37p to 68p (printed no.58)   6.00   ☐

2002 Four Regions (4th July)

This pack is the first to contain stamps of England, Scotland, Wales and Northern Ireland together. Inside is some attractive photography to represent each country. Contains four stamps of 68p value.

PPD83   2002 Four Regions (printed no.59)   6.00   ☐

2002 Wilding's Collection I (5th December)

This pack commemorates the 50th Anniversary of the first stamps to bear an image of The Queen, and tells the story of how Dorothy Wilding's photographs were incorporated onto the stamps. Contains a miniature sheet of nine stamps from 1p to 50p, 2nd Class and 1st Class.

PPD84   2002 Wilding's Collection I (printed no.59)   32.00   ☐

2003 Universal European (27th March)

This pack contains a set of low value definitives. Inside tells of Machin's detailed sculpture of the Queen and how it was incorporated onto the stamps. Contains two Airmail stamps; one for Europe and one Worldwide.

PPD85   2003 Universal European (printed no.60)   5.50   ☐

2003 Wilding's Collection II (20th May)

This issue follows-on from the 2002 Wilding's Collection I pack and tells of the difficulty in achieving satisfactory print colours on the stamps. Contains a miniature sheet of nine stamps from 4p to 68p, and Europe.

PPD86   2003 Wilding's Collection II (printed no.61)   8.00   ☐

2003 Machin £1.50 to £5 (1st July)

This pack contains a set of high value definitives. Inside tells of Machin's detailed sculpture of the Queen and how it was incorporated onto the stamps. Contains four stamps from £1.50 to £5.

PPD87   2003 Machin £1.50 to £5 (printed no.62)   22.00   ☐

2003 England (14th October)

This Country pack celebrates the diversity of England's landscape. It includes some attractive photography and discusses the influence of English flora. Contains four stamps from 2nd Class to 68p.

PPD88   2003 England (printed no.63)   5.00   ☐

2003 Scotland (14th October)

This Country pack commemorates Scotland's first elected Parliament in almost 300 years. It includes some attractive photography and information on Scotland's geology. Contains four stamps from 2nd Class to 68p.

PPD89   2003 Scotland (printed no.64)   6.00   ☐

2003 Wales (14th October)

This Country pack commemorates the creation of the Welsh National Assembly with some attractive photography. Written in English and Welsh. Contains four stamps from 2nd Class to 68p.

PPD90   2003 Wales (printed no.65)   6.00   ☐

2003 Northern Ireland (14th October)

This Country pack heralds a new era for Northern Ireland. It includes some attractive photography and information on Northern Ireland's rural landscape. Contains four stamps from 2nd Class to 68p.

PPD91   2003 Northern Ireland (printed no.66)   6.00   ☐

2004 World, 1st, 7p to 43p (1st April)

This pack contains a set of low value definitives. Inside tells of Machin's detailed sculpture of The Queen and how it was incorporated onto the stamps. Contains seven stamps from 7p to 43p, Worldwide and 1st Class.

PPD92   2004 World, 1st, 7p to 43p (printed no.67)   8.00   ☐

2004 Four Regions (11th May)

This pack features stamps of England, Scotland, Wales and Northern Ireland together. Inside is some attractive photography to represent each country. Contains four stamps of 40p value.

PPD93   2004 Four Regions (printed no.68)   7.50   ☐

2005 The Castles Definitives (22nd March)

Commemorating the 50th Anniversary of Lynton Lamb's 'Castles' stamp designs, approved by The Queen in March 1955, this pack also features some of the other Artists who submitted designs and shows pictures of their work. Contains four stamps from 50p to £1.

PPD94 2005 The Castles Definitives (printed no.69) 6.00 ☐

2005 Four Regions (5th April)

This pack features stamps of England, Scotland, Wales and Northern Ireland. Inside is some attractive photography to represent each country. Contains four stamps of 42p value.

PPD95 2005 Four Regions (printed no.70) 7.50 ☐

2005 World, Europe, 1st, 2nd, 1p to £1 (6th Sept)

This pack contains a set of low value definitives. Inside tells of Machin's detailed sculpture of The Queen and how it was incorporated onto the stamps. Contains 19 stamps from 1p to £1, Worldwide, Europe, 2nd Class and 1st Class.

PPD96 2005 World, Europe, 1st, 2nd, 1p to £1 (printed no.71) 35.00 ☐

2006 Machin 37p to 72p (28th March)

This pack contains a set of low value definitives. Inside tells of Machin's detailed sculpture of The Queen and how it was incorporated onto the stamps. Contains four stamps from 37p to 72p.

PPD97 2006 Machin 37p to 72p (printed no.72) 9.00 ☐

2006 Four Regions (28th March)

This pack features stamps of England, Scotland, Wales and Northern Ireland. Inside is some attractive photography to represent each country. Contains four sets of two stamps of 44p and 72p.

PPD98 2006 Four Regions (printed no.73) 9.00 ☐

2006 Machin - Pricing In Proportion (1st August)

Featuring a new style, this pack includes 21 images that show the development of Arnold Machin's coinage and stamp designs, which were originally based on the Penny Black. Contains six stamps from 12p to 1st Class Large.

PPD99 2006 Machin - Pricing In Proportion (printed no.74) 6.00 ☐

2007 Machin, 16p to 78p (27th March)

This pack includes 21 images that show the development of Arnold Machin's coinage and stamp designs, which were originally based on the Penny Black. Contains five stamps from 16p to 78p.

PPD100 2007 Machin, 16p to 78p (printed no.75)   8.00   ☐

2007 Four Regions (27th March)

This pack features stamps of England, Scotland, Wales and Northern Ireland. Inside is some attractive photography to represent each country. Contains four sets of two stamps of 48p and 78p.

PPD101 2007 Four Regions (printed no.76)   10.00   ☐

2007 40th Anniversary Machin (5th June)

This pack includes 21 images that show the development of Arnold Machin's coinage and stamp designs, which were originally based on the Penny Black. Contains 20 stamps from 1p to Worldwide.

PPD102 2007 40th Anniversary Machin
(printed no.77)   25.00   ☐

2008 Machin 15p to 81p (1st April)

This pack includes 21 images that show the development of Arnold Machin's coinage and stamp designs, which were originally based on the Penny Black. Contains three stamps from 15p to 81p.

PPD103 2008 Machin 15p to 81p (printed no.78)   5.00   ☐

2008 Four Regions (1st April)

This pack features stamps of England, Scotland, Wales and Northern Ireland. Inside is some attractive photography to represent each country. Contains four sets of two stamps of 50p and 81p.

PPD104 2008 Four Regions (printed no.79)   9.00   ☐

2008 Country Definitives (29th September)

Commemorating the 50th Anniversary of the Country Definitives. A very decorative pack featuring pictures of selected, and unselected, stamp designs including those for Guernsey, Jersey and Isle of Man. Contains a miniature sheet of stamps replicating original designs.

PPD105 2008 Country Definitives (printed no.80)   11.00   ☐

2008 Four Regions Pictorial (29th September)

This pack features stamps of England, Scotland, Wales and Northern Ireland. Inside is some attractive photography to represent each country. Contains four sets of four stamps from 2nd Class to 81p.

PPD106 2008 Four Regions Pictorial (printed no.81)   30.00   ☐

2009 Machin 2nd to £1 (17th February)

This pack includes 21 images that show the development of Arnold Machin's coinage and stamp designs, which were originally based on the Penny Black. Contains six self-adhesive stamps from 2nd Class to £1.

PPD107 2009 Machin 2nd to £1 (printed no.82)   7.00   ☐

2009 Machin £1.50 to £5.00 (17th February)

This pack includes 21 images that show the development of Arnold Machin's coinage and stamp designs, which were originally based on the Penny Black. Contains four self-adhesive stamps from £1.50 to £5.

PPD108 2009 Machin £1.50 to £5.00
(printed no.83)   25.00   ☐

2009 Machin 17p to 90p (31st March)

This pack includes 21 images that show the development of Arnold Machin's coinage and stamp designs, which were originally based on the Penny Black. Contains four stamps from 17p to 90p.

PPD109 2009 Machin 17p to 90p (printed no.84)   7.00   ☐

2009 Four Regions (31st March)

This pack features stamps of England, Scotland, Wales and Northern Ireland. Inside is some attractive photography to represent each country. Contains four sets of two stamps of 56p and 90p.

PPD110 2009 Four Regions (printed no.85)   11.00   ☐

2010 Machin 60p to £1.46, E, World, 1st Class Large Recorded (30th March)

This pack includes 21 images that show the development of Arnold Machin's coinage and stamp designs, which were originally based on the Penny Black. Contains nine stamps from 60p to 1st Class Large Recorded.

PPD111 2010 Machin 60p to £1.46, E, World,
1st Class Large Recorded (printed no.86)   17.50   ☐

2010 Four Regions (30th March)

This pack features stamps of England, Scotland, Wales and Northern Ireland. Inside is some attractive photography to represent each country. Contains four sets of two stamps of 60p and 97p.

PPD112   2010 Four Regions (printed no.87)   11.00   ☐

2010 Machin Collectors (8th March)

This pack includes 21 images that show the development of Arnold Machin's coinage and stamp designs, which were originally based on the Penny Black. Contains 24 stamps from 1p to Worldwide.

PPD113   2010 Machin Collectors (printed no.88)   32.00   ☐

2010 Machin Special Delivery Stamps (26th Oct)

This pack includes 21 images that show the development of Arnold Machin's coinage and stamp designs, which were originally based on the Penny Black. Contains two self-adhesive Special Delivery stamps; up to 100g and up to 500g.

PPD114   2010 Machin Special Delivery Stamps
              (printed no.89)   20.00   ☐

2011 Machin 1p to £1.65 (29th March)

This pack includes 21 images that show the development of Arnold Machin's coinage and stamp designs, which were originally based on the Penny Black. Contains nine self-adhesive stamps from 1p to £1.65.

PPD115   2011 Machin 1p to £1.65 (printed no.90)   15.00   ☐

2011 Four Regions (29th March)

This pack features stamps of England, Scotland, Wales and Northern Ireland. Inside is some attractive photography to represent each country. Contains four sets of two stamps of 68p and £1.10.

PPD116   2011 Four Regions (printed no.91)   14.00   ☐

2012 The Olympic and Paralympic Games
(5th January)

In advance of the 30th Olympiad, this pack contains facts and figures on previous Games and looks forward to London 2012. It also includes information on the distinctive emblem, which is featured on the stamps. Contains four self-adhesive stamps from 1st Class to Worldwide.

PPD117   2012 The Olympic and Paralympic Games
              (printed no.92)   8.00   ☐

2012 Diamond Jubilee (6th February)

To commemorate the Queen's Diamond Jubilee, this attractive pack contains a wealth of information on the use of Her image on stamps, coinage and banknotes. It also includes a brief resumé of each of the six artists involved in their design. Contains a miniature sheet of six 1st Class stamps.

PPD118 2012 Diamond Jubilee (printed no.93)	10.00	☐

2012 Machin 1st Class to £1.90 (25th April)

This pack includes 21 images that show the development of Arnold Machin's coinage and stamp designs, which were originally based on the Penny Black. Contains five self-adhesive stamps from 1st Class to £1.90.

PPD119 2012 Machin 1st Class to £1.90 (printed no.94)	10.00	☐

2012 Four Regions (25th April)

This pack features stamps of England, Scotland, Wales and Northern Ireland. Inside is some attractive photography to represent each country. Contains four sets of two stamps of 87p and £1.28.

PPD120 2012 Four Regions (printed no.95)	14.00	☐

2013 Machin 1p to £1 & 1st Large (3rd January)

This pack includes 21 images that show the development of Arnold Machin's coinage and stamp designs, which were originally based on the Penny Black. Contains nine self-adhesive stamps from 1p to £1, 1st Class and 1st Class Large.

PPD121 2013 Machin 1p to £1 & 1st Large (printed no.96)	8.00	☐

2013 Machin 78p to £1.88 & Signed For (27th March)

This pack includes 21 images that show the development of Arnold Machin's coinage and stamp designs, which were originally based on the Penny Black. Contains five self-adhesive stamps from 78p to £1.88 and 1st Class Large Signed For.

PPD122 2013 Machin 78p to £1.88 & Signed For (printed no.97)	14.50	☐

2013 Four Regions (27th March)

This pack features stamps of England, Scotland, Wales and Northern Ireland. Inside is some attractive photography to represent each country. Contains four stamps of 88p value.

PPD123 2013 Four Regions (printed no.98)	7.00	☐

Collectors Club

These rare packs were given to members of The Collectors Club, which was set up to promote stamp collecting to children and as a family activity. It became one of the largest clubs of its kind with 70,000 members worldwide.

Only three presentation packs were issued specifically for The Collectors Club and they are now difficult to obtain.

2000 Queen Mother's 100th Birthday (4th August)

Issued to mark the occasion of The Queen Mother's 100th birthday, this pack offered collectors a unique way to keep and display the specially produced, commemorative miniature sheet.

Inside the Pack

PPC1   2000 Queen Mother's 100th Birthday   100.00 ☐

2002 Circus (10th April)

This fun pack contains a set of the 2001 Circus stamps and a pop-out spinning disc game.

Inside the Pack

PPC2   2002 Circus   100.00 ☐

2003 Occasions (4th February)

This Collectors Club Pack was produced for the 2003 Occasions stamp issue and contains a fact sheet about Valentine's day. The stamps were designed to be interactive; each stamp has three tick boxes for the sender to choose the most appropriate message.

Inside the Pack

PPC3   2003 Occasions   100.00 ☐

Forerunner Packs

Considered by many to be the first presentation packs issued, Forerunners are now very scarce. Due to their age, a slight crinkling of the pack, around the edges and the window, is normal.

Original packs were sold sealed and retain a higher market value. The guide prices listed in this catalogue are for sealed packs. If a pack has been opened carefully, its value might be 30% lower.

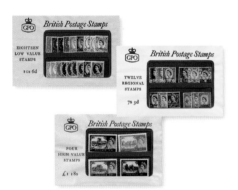

1960 DLR Castles (9th July)

A forerunner pack for sale in the UK and USA, inscribed with £1 18s or $6.50 accordingly, containing a complete set of the high value, permanent issue, stamps of Great Britain. Contains four stamps from 2/6 to £1.

PPF1a	1960 DLR Castles UK	1750.00	☐
PPF1b	1960 DLR Castles USA	3000.00	☐
PPF1c	1960 DLR Castles. No price on front	5000.00	☐

1960 Phosphor Graphites (9th July)

A forerunner pack for sale in the UK and USA, inscribed with 3s 8d or 50c accordingly, contains two complete sets of the low value, permanent issue, stamps produced for use with the experimental model of the British Automatic Letter Facer. The stamps bear lines of graphite and phosphor to enable the machine first to detect the stamps and then to arrange the letters in stacks, with the stamps in the same corner. Contains two sets of eight stamps from ½d to 4½d.

PPF2a	1960 Phosphor Graphites UK	275.00	☐
PPF2b	1960 Phosphor Graphites USA	325.00	☐

CORRECTION. The ½d, 1d & 1½d stamps bear the St. Edward Crown Royal Cypher watermark.

Also exists with a 'Correction' sticker

1960 Wildings (9th July)

A forerunner pack for sale in the UK and USA, inscribed with 10s 6d or $1.80 accordingly, containing a complete set of the low value, permanent issue, stamps of Great Britain. The stamps are in five different designs, all based on the rose of England, the daffodil of Wales, the thistle of Scotland and the shamrock of Northern Ireland. Contains 18 stamps from ½d to 1/6.

| PPF3a | 1960 Wildings UK | 300.00 | ☐ |
| PPF3b | 1960 Wildings USA | 400.00 | ☐ |

1960 Regionals (9th July)

A forerunner pack for sale in the UK and USA, inscribed with 7s 3d or $1.20 accordingly, containing a complete set of stamps issued for the different countries of the United Kingdom. Contains four sets of three stamps from 1/3 to 6d.

| PPF4a | 1960 Regionals UK | 300.00 | ☐ |
| PPF4b | 1960 Regionals USA | 400.00 | ☐ |

Format Packs

These packs are specialist products that contain stamp issues in blocks of varying formats. Sold at face value, they were available from the Philatelic Bureau and selected Post Offices.

It is thought that in the majority of cases the stamps were removed and the pack discarded. This has led to there being very few complete format packs available, giving them a comparitively high market value.

The packs in this section have not been allocated a catalogue number as there might be others uncovered that, when interspersed chronologically, would void a sequential numbering system.

1998 Endangered Species (20th January)

A set of six packs, each one containing gutter pairs of stamps from the 1998 Endangered Species commemorative issue. Also available in cylinder block format. This set contains: Common dormouse 20p, Lady's slipper orchid 26p, Song thrush 31p, Shining ram's-horn snail 37p, Mole cricket 43p, Devil's bolete 63p.

| 1998 | Endangered Species - Gutter Pairs (6 packs) | 600.00 | ☐ |
| 1998 | Endangered Species - Cylinder Block (6 packs) | 600.00 | ☐ |

1998 Lighthouses (24th March)

A set of five packs, each one containing a cylinder block of six stamps from the 1999 Lighthouses commemorative issue. This set contains: St. John's Point 20p, The Smalls 26p, Needles Rocks 37p, Bell Rock 43p, Eddystone 63p.

| 1998 | Lighthouses - Cylinder Block (5 packs) | 500.00 | ☐ |

1998 Comedians (23rd April)

A set of five packs, each one containing a quarter sheet of 25 stamps from the 1998 Comedians commemorative issue. Also available in gutter pairs and cylinder block format.

One pack containing a Quarter Sheet of stamps

1998	Comedians - Quarter Sheet (5 packs)	900.00	☐
1998	Comedians - Gutter Pairs (5 packs)	500.00	☐
1998	Comedians - Cylinder Block (5 packs)	500.00	☐

1998 Magical Worlds (21st July)

A set of five packs, each one containing a cylinder block of six stamps from the 1998 Magical Worlds commemorative issue. Also available in gutter pairs format. This set contains: The Hobbit 20p, The Lion, the Witch and the Wardrobe 26p, The Phoenix and the Carpet 37p, The Borrowers 43p, Through the Looking Glass 63p.

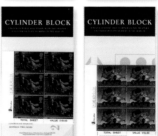

| 1998 | Magical Worlds - Cylinder Block (5 packs) | 500.00 | ☐ |
| 1998 | Magical Worlds - Gutter Pairs (5 packs) | 500.00 | ☐ |

1998 Carnival (25th August)

A set of four packs, each one containing two gutter pairs of stamps from the 1998 Carnival commemorative issue. This set contains: Woman in Yellow Feathered Costume 20p, Woman in Blue Costume and Head-dress 26p, Group of Children in White and Gold 43p, Child in 'Tree' Costume 63p.

1998 Carnival (4 packs)   350.00 ☐

1998 Speed (29th September)

A set of five packs, each one containing two gutter pairs of stamps from the 1998 Speed commemorative issue. This set contains: Sir Malcolm Campbell's Bluebird 20p, Sir Henry Seagrave's Sunbeam 26p, John G. Parry Thomas's Babs 30p, John R. Cobb's Railton Mobil Special, Donald Campbell's Bluebird CN7 63p.

1998 Speed (5 packs)   400.00 ☐

1999 Inventors' Tale (12th January)

A single pack containing a cylinder block of six stamps from the 1999 Inventors' Tale issue. This pack contains: Timekeeping 20p.

Note: The other three stamps in this issue might also have been available in a Format Pack, but we are not aware of any in circulation at the time of publishing.

1999 Inventors' Tale (1 pack)   100.00 ☐

1999 Patients' Tale (2nd March)

A single pack containing three gutter pairs of stamps from the 1999 Patients' Tale issue. This pack contains: Jenner's vaccination 20p.

Note: The other three stamps in this issue might also have been available in a Format Pack, but we are not aware of any in circulation at the time of publishing.

1999 Patients' Tale (1 pack)   100.00 ☐

1999 Settlers' Tale (6th April)

A single pack containing a cylinder block of six stamps from the 1999 Settlers' Tale issue. This pack contains: Pilgrim Fathers and Red Indian 26p.

Note: The other three stamps in this issue might also have been available in a Format Pack, but we are not aware of any in circulation at the time of publishing.

1999 Settlers' Tale (1 pack)   100.00 ☐

1999 Scientists' Tale (3rd August)

A set of four packs, each one containing three gutter pairs of stamps from the 1999 Scientists' Tale commemorative issue. This set contains: Molecular Structures 19p, Galapagos Finch and Fossilised Skeleton 26p, Rotation of Polarised Light by Magnetism 44p, Saturn 64p.

1999 Scientists' Tale (4 packs)	400.00 ☐

1999 Solar Eclipse (11th August)

Celebrating the Hubble space telescope, named after astronomer Edwin Powel Hubble, which was launched to obtain better photographs of the planets. Contains a miniature sheet of four stamps.

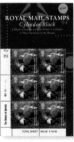

1999 Solar Eclipse	60.00 ☐

1999 Millennium Timekeeper (14th December)

To commemorate the Millennium, the stamps in this pack are based on Earth's rotation and hands of a clock. As the continents pass, the clock's hands draw closer together until, at the moment of the Millennium, they coincide. Contains a miniature sheet of four stamps.

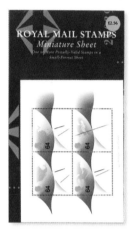

1999 Millennium Timekeeper	60.00 ☐

2000 Above and Beyond (18th January)

A set of four packs, each one containing a cylinder block of six stamps from the 2000 Above and Beyond commemorative pack. This set contains: Barn Owl 19p, Night Sky 26p, River Goyt & Textile Mills 44p, Cape Gannets 64p.

2000 Above and Beyond (4 packs)	400.00 ☐

2000 Fire and Light (1st February)

A set of four packs, each one containing a cylinder block of six stamps from the 2000 Fire and Light commemorative issue. This set contains: Millenium Beacon 19p, Garratt Steam Locomotive 26p, Lightning 44p, Multicoloured Lights 64p.

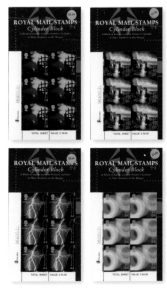

2000 Fire and Light (4 packs)	400.00 ☐

2000 Water and Coast (7th March)

A single pack containing a cylinder block of six stamps from the 2000 Water and Coast issue. This pack contains: Frog's Legs and Water Lilies 26p.

Note: The other three stamps in this issue might also have been available in a Format Pack, but we are not aware of any in circulation at the time of publishing.

2000 Water and Coast (1 pack)	100.00 ☐

2000 Life and Earth (4th April)

A set of four packs, each one containing a cylinder block of six stamps from the 2000 Life and Earth commemorative issue. This set contains: Reed Beds River Braid 2nd Class, South American Leaf-cutter Ants 1st Class, Solar Sensors 44p, Hydroponic Leaves 64p.

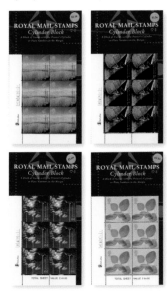

2000 Life and Earth (4 packs)	400.00 ☐

2000 Art and Craft (2nd May)

A set of four packs, each one containing a cylinder block of six stamps from the 2000 Art and Craft commemorative issue. This set contains: Pottery Glaze 2nd Class, Bankside Galleries 1st Class, Road Marking 45p, People of Salford 65p.

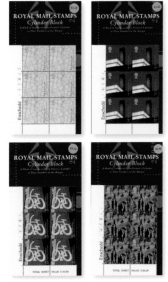

2000 Art and Craft (4 packs)	400.00 ☐

2000 Matthews Palette (22nd May)

Produced to mark the Stamp Show 2000, International Stamp Exhibition, which was held in London. The stamps feature Jeffery Matthews' colour palette. Contains a miniature sheet of eight stamps.

2000 Matthews Palette	60.00 ☐

2000 Her Majesty's Stamp Show (23rd May)

This issue was produced on the occasion of the Stamp Show 2000. Contains a miniature sheet of four 1st Class stamps and one special £1 stamp.

2000 Her Majesty's Stamp Show	60.00 ☐

2000 People and Place (6th June)

A set of four packs, each one containing a cylinder block of six stamps from the 2000 People and Place commemorative issue. This set contains: Children playing 2nd Class, Millennium Bridge 1st Class, Daisies 45p, African Hut and Thatched Cottage 65p.

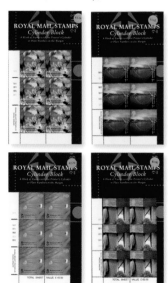

2000 People and Place (4 packs)	400.00 ☐

2000 Stone and Soil (4th July)

A set of four packs, each one containing a cylinder block of six stamps from the 2000 Stone and Soil commemorative issue. This set contains: Raising the Stone 2nd Class, Horses Hooves 1st Class, Cyclist 45p, Bluebell Wood 65p.

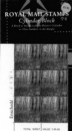

2000 Stone and Soil (4 packs)	400.00 ☐

2000 Tree and Leaf (1st August)

A set of four packs, each one containing a cylinder block of six stamps from the 2000 Tree and Leaf commemorative issue. This set contains: Tree Roots 2nd Class, Sunflower 1st Class, Sycamore Seeds 45p, Forest, Doire Dach 65p.

2000 Tree and Leaf (4 packs)	400.00	☐

2000 Mind and Matter (5th September)

A set of four packs, each one containing a cylinder block of six stamps from the 2000 Mind and Matter commemorative issue. This set contains: Head of Gigantios 2nd Class, Gathering Water Lilies 1st Class, X-ray 45p, Tartan Wool Holder 65p.

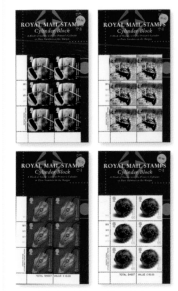

2000 Mind and Matter (4 packs)	400.00	☐

2000 Queen Mother's Birthday (4th August)

Celebrating the momentous 100th birthday of HM Queen Elizabeth, the Queen Mother. Contains a miniature sheet of four stamps that each portray a member of the Royal family; HM The Queen, HRH The Prince of Wales, HRH Prince William and the Queen Mother.

2000 Queen Mother's Birthday	70.00	☐

2001 Occasions Special Edition (3rd July)

Very scarce and unusual packs. Each one contains 10 1st Class stamps from the 2001 Occasions presentation pack. This set contains five packs of 10 stamps (50 stamps in total): New Baby, Love & Romance, Thanks, Occasions, New Home.

2001 Occasions Special Edition (5 packs)	240.00	☐

2003 Fun Fruit & Veg - Standard (25th March)

A pack of fun, shaped, stamps and stickers. Contains 10 1st Class self-adhesive stamps of popular fruit and vegetables, plus 76 'character building' stickers of eyes, mouths, hats, shoes and many more.

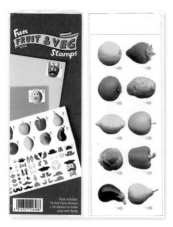

2003 Fun Fruit & Veg 12.50 ☐

2003 Fun Fruit & Veg - Supermarket (25th March)

A pack of fun, shaped, stamps and stickers produced with a punch hole for display in supermarkets. Contains 10 1st Class self-adhesive stamps of popular fruit and vegetables, plus 76 'character building' stickers of eyes, mouths, hats, shoes and many more.

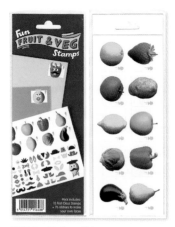

2003 Fun Fruit and Veg 15.00 ☐

2010 Accession of King George V (8th May)

A set of four packs commemorating 100 years since King George V acceded to the throne. The day of his accession was also the 70th Anniversary of the Penny Black. This set contains a Gutter Pair, Cylinder Block, Traffic Lights and Corner Inscription 1st Class stamps.

2010 Accession of King George V (4 packs) 120.00 ☐

2010 Britain Alone - Dunkirk (13th May)

Produced solely for London 2010 Festival of Stamps, this set of four packs contains Gutter Pairs, Cylinder Block, Traffic Lights and Top Left stamps. Each pack contains a full issue of 2010 Britain Alone stamps.

2010 Britain Alone - Dunkirk (4 packs) 600.00 ☐

Greetings Packs

These packs were produced annually from 1992 to 1997
and contained 'Greetings' stamps that were also available in
booklets. Each pack contains 10 1st Class stamps and a set of
corresponding labels.

1992 Greetings - Memories (28th January)

This attractive pack depicts a personal collection of photos, letters and postcards to evoke happy memories. The stamps are presented as a sheet that, when whole, is a single picture of memorabilia. Contains 10 pictorial 1st Class stamps and a set of corresponding Greetings labels.

PPG1   1992 Greetings - Memories (printed no.G1) 10.00   ☐

1993 Greetings - Giving (2nd February)

This fully illustrated pack celebrates the act of Giving by using pictures of well-known characters from children's stories. The stamps are presented as a sheet of characters giving or receiving something. Contains 10 pictorial 1st Class stamps and a set of corresponding Greetings labels.

PPG2   1993 Greetings - Giving (printed no.G2)   10.00   ☐

1994 Greetings - Messages (2nd February)

This colourful pack holds a reminder of much-loved children's books and fictional characters in the form of a fully illustrated short story. The stamps are presented as a sheet of characters sending or receiving a message. Contains 10 pictorial 1st Class stamps and a set of corresponding Greetings labels.

PPG3   1994 Greetings - Messages (printed no.G3) 10.00   ☐

1995 Greetings - Art (21st March)

A greeting is usually an expression of goodwill and this pack tells of many ways it might be communicated, from ancient dance to the modern cheek-kiss. The stamps are presented as a sheet of artworks. Contains 10 pictorial 1st Class stamps and a set of corresponding Greetings labels.

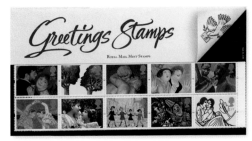

PPG4   1995 Greetings - Art (printed no.G4)   10.00   ☐

1996 Greetings - Cartoons (28th January)

Celebrating the art of cartoons, this pack points out the many forms they can take, from satirical to surreal. The stamps are presented as a sheet of amusing cartoons. Contains 10 illustrated 1st Class stamps and a set of corresponding Greetings labels.

PPG5   1996 Greetings - Cartoons (printed no.G5) 11.00   ☐

1997 Greetings - Flowers (28th January)

A beautifully illustrated pack which celebrates botanical art in all its glory, especially the work of G D Ehret who was commissioned to illustrate the specimens discovered on Captain Cook's voyage to Newfoundland. Contains 10 illustrated 1st Class stamps and a set of corresponding Greetings labels.

PPG6   1997 Greetings - Flowers (printed no.G6)   10.00   ☐

Miniature Sheet Collection Packs

Annual production of these collection packs began in 2005.
Presented in durable plastic folders, they contain a complete
set of the year's British stamp miniature sheets with an
accompanying information card.

2005 Miniature Sheet Collection Pack

From pageantry and royal romance to drama on the high seas.
A Collection Pack containing all the miniature sheets issued
throughout 2005.

Some of the
Pack contents

| PPM1 | 2005 Miniature Sheet Collection Pack | 70.00 | ☐ |

2006 Miniature Sheet Collection Pack

From engineering genius to courage under fire. A Collection Pack
containing all the miniature sheets issued throughout 2006.

Some of the
Pack contents

| PPM2 | 2006 Miniature Sheet Collection Pack | 70.00 | ☐ |

2007 Miniature Sheet Collection Pack

From million-selling discs to a heavenly choir of angels.
A Collection Pack containing all the miniature sheets issued
throughout 2007.

Some of the
Pack contents

| PPM3 | 2007 Miniature Sheet Collection Pack | 70.00 | ☐ |

2008 Miniature Sheet Collection Pack

From tales of espionage and adventure to awe-inspiring
architecture. A Collection Pack containing all the miniature
sheets issued throughout 2008.

Some of the
Pack contents

| PPM4 | 2008 Miniature Sheet Collection Pack | 54.00 | ☐ |

2009 Miniature Sheet Collection Pack

From the birth of a poet to a round-the-world voyage of wonder. A Collection Pack containing all the miniature sheets issued throughout 2009.

Some of the Pack contents

| PPM5 | 2009 Miniature Sheet Collection Pack | 62.00 | ☐ |

2010 Miniature Sheet Collection Pack

From the accession of King George V to Christmas with Wallace and Gromit. A Collection Pack containing all the miniature sheets issued throughout 2010.

Some of the Pack contents

| PPM6 | 2010 Miniature Sheet Collection Pack | 54.00 | ☐ |

2011 Miniature Sheet Collection Pack

From the UK's first lenticular stamps to the 400th Anniversary of the King James Bible. A Collection Pack containing all the miniature sheets issued throughout 2011.

Some of the Pack contents

| PPM7 | 2011 Miniature Sheet Collection Pack | 120.00 | ☐ |

2012 Miniature Sheet Collection Pack

Celebrating the best of British from the Diamond Jubilee to the Olympic and Paralympic Games. A Collection Pack containing all the miniature sheets issued throughout 2012.

Some of the Pack contents

| PPM8 | 2012 Miniature Sheet Collection Pack | 55.00 | ☐ |

2013 Miniature Sheet Collection Pack

Celebrating British achievements in sport, art and design, transport, locomotion and popular culture. A Collection Pack containing all the miniature sheets issued throughout 2013.

Some of the Pack contents

PPM9   2013 Miniature Sheet Collection Pack   50.00   ☐

Postage Due Packs

Four presentation packs were issued by the Post Office containing Postage Due (To Pay) labels - the first in 1971 and the last in 1994. All the packs include information on the background of 'To Pay' labels, which were introduced to Great Britain in 1914.

1971 Postage Dues (3rd November)

This pack tells the history of surcharging on underpaid post and of the introduction of 'postage due' labels on 20th April 1914. It also illustrates the original labels. Contains 10 stamps from ½p to £1.

| PPT1 | 1971 Postage Dues | 30.00 | ☐ |

1977 Postage Dues (30th March)

This pack tells the history of surcharging on underpaid post and of the introduction of 'postage due' labels on 20th April 1914. It also illustrates the original labels. Contains 12 stamps from 4p to £1.

| PPT2 | 1977 Postage Dues | 14.00 | ☐ |

1982 Postage Dues (9th June)

This year saw a redesigned pack and labels, to bring them in line with the Post Office Corporate Identity of the time. Inside tells the history of surcharging on underpaid post and of the introduction of 'postage due' labels on 20th April 1914. It also illustrates the original labels. Contains 12 stamps from 1p to £5.

| PPT3 | 1982 Postage Dues | 32.00 | ☐ |

1994 Postage Dues (15th February)

In 1994, Royal Mail redesigned their pack and labels to bring them in line with their branding of the time and reinforce their long-standing royal connection. Inside tells the history of surcharging on underpaid post and of the introduction of 'postage due' labels on 20th April 1914. It also illustrates the previous label designs. Contains nine stamps from 1p to £5 which feature an embossed image of the St. Edward's Crown.

| PPT4 | 1994 Postage Dues | 40.00 | ☐ |

Post & Go Packs

Post & Go Packs were introduced in 2009 and have proved
popular. They comprise a set of self-adhesive stamps on a
simple carrier and information card. Royal Mail issue these
packs regularly throughout the year.

2009 Post & Go Stamps (31st March)

Following a new generation of self-service postage machines, trialled in 2008, this is the first pack of its type. Developed as a more convenient way to buy postage, the machine overprinted one of five common letter rates on demand. Contains five stamps from 1st Class to Worldwide up to 20g.

PPP1   2009 Post & Go Stamps   70.00   ☐

2010 Birds of Britain I (17th September)

This is the first in a series of pictorial Post & Go packs, featuring six birds commonly seen in UK gardens. There is a brief description of each bird with its scientific name and picture of its egg. Contains six self-adhesive 1st Class stamps.

PPP2   2010 Birds of Britain I   17.50   ☐

2011 Birds of Britain II (24th January)

The second in the series of pictorial Birds of Britain packs, featuring six birds commonly seen in UK gardens. There is a brief description of each bird with its scientific name and picture of its egg. Contains six self-adhesive 1st Class stamps.

PPP3 2011 Birds of Britain II   45.00   ☐

2011 Birds of Britain III (19th May)

The third in the series of pictorial Birds of Britain packs, featuring six waterland birds commonly seen in the UK. There is a brief description of each bird with its scientific name and picture of its egg. Contains six self-adhesive 1st Class stamps.

PPP4 2011 Birds of Britain III   8.00   ☐

2011 Birds of Britain IV (16th September)

This is the fourth and last of the Birds of Britain packs, featuring six seabirds commonly found around the UK's coasts. There is a brief description of each bird with its scientific name and picture of its egg. Contains six self-adhesive 1st Class stamps.

PPP5   2011 Birds of Britain IV   8.00   ☐

2012 Farm Animals I - Sheep (24th February)

Starting a new series of pictorial Post & Go packs, this one features six breeds of sheep. There is a brief description of each breed and its wool. Contains six self-adhesive 1st Class stamps.

PPP6   2012 Farm Animals I - Sheep
        (printed no. P&G 6)   7.00   ☐
Also exists with the strip of stamps cut in the wrong place, meaning the image doesn't match the description underneath

2012 **Farm Animals II - Pigs** (24th April)

The second in the series of British Farm Animals, this pack features six breeds of pig. There is a brief description of each breed and its history. Contains six self-adhesive 1st Class stamps.

| PPP7 | 2012 Farm Animals II - Pigs (printed no. P&G 7) | 7.00 | ☐ |

2012 **Farm Animals III - Cattle** (28th September)

The third and last in the series of British Farm Animals, this pack features six breeds of cattle. There is a brief description of each breed and its history. Contains six self-adhesive 1st Class stamps.

| PPP9 | 2012 Farm Animals III - Cattle (printed no. P&G 9) | 6.00 | ☐ |

2012 **Union Flag** (21st May)

This pack features an illustration by Anton Morris which first appeared on the Flags miniature sheet issued in 2001 as part of the Centenary of the Royal Navy Submarine Service stamp set. Contains a self-adhesive 1st Class stamp.

| PPP8 | 2012 Union Flag (printed no. P&G 8) | 2.50 | ☐ |

2013 **2nd Class & 2nd Class Large** (20th February)

With the introduction of the stamps in this pack, self-service postage machines were able to overprint eight of the most popular tariff values. Contains two self-adhesive 2nd Class stamps.

| PPP10 | 2013 2nd Class & 2nd Class Large (printed no. P&G 10) | 3.00 | ☐ |

2013 Freshwater Life I - Ponds (22nd February)

The first in another series of pictorial Post & Go packs, featuring a variety of common, and endangered, pond wildlife. There is a brief description of each species and its habitat. Contains six self-adhesive 1st Class stamps.

| PPP11 | 2013 Freshwater Life I - Ponds (printed no. P&G 11) | 7.00 | ☐ |

2013 Freshwater Life III - Rivers (20th September)

The third and last in the series of Freshwater Life, this pack features five fish and a fly larva that live in rivers. There is a brief description of each species and its habitat. Contains six self-adhesive 1st Class stamps.

| PPP13 | 2013 Freshwater Life III - Rivers (printed no. P&G 13) | 7.00 | ☐ |

2013 Freshwater Life II - Lakes (25th June)

The second in the series of Freshwater Life, this pack features six creatures that live in Britain's lakes. There is a brief description of each species and its habitat. Contains six self-adhesive 1st Class stamps.

| PPP12 | 2013 Freshwater Life II - Lakes (printed no. P&G 12) | 7.00 | ☐ |

2014 British Flora I - Spring Blooms (19th February)

The first in a new series of pictorial Post & Go packs, featuring a variety of springtime flowers. There is a brief description of each species and its growing habits. Contains six self-adhesive 1st Class stamps.

| PPP14 | 2014 British Flora I - Spring Blooms (printed no. P&G 14) | 7.00 | ☐ |

Reproduction Packs

These fascinating packs contain reproductions of significant British stamp issues, which are sometimes printed using the original die.

The most elusive of these packs is the 2000 Penny Black (PPR1), which commands a significant premium over its original issue price.

2000 Penny Black (1st January)

160 years after the first Penny Black appeared, this pack contains information about the original printing process. Contains a block of four reproduction stamps, hand-printed from an original metal die.

| PPR1 | 2000 Penny Black | 75.00 | ☐ |

2010 Postal Union Congress (8th May)

This pack includes images and information about the 9th Postal Union Congress, held in London in 1929, and development of the Congress stamp. Contains a block of four reproduction stamps.

| PPR2 | 2010 Postal Union Congress | 9.00 | ☐ |

2011 Penny Red Anniversary (15th September)

Marking the 170th Anniversary of the Penny Red, this pack tells the interesting story of Rowland Hill's determination to prevent any reuse of Penny Black stamps by way of a Cancellation. Contains a block of four reproduction stamps.

| PPR3 | 2011 Penny Red Anniversary | 9.00 | ☐ |

2012 Olympic Games 1948 (27th July)

Commemorating the previous time that the Games were held in London, this pack is full of information and pictures about the designs submitted for the 1948 Olympic Games Stamps and the artists that created them. Contains a block of four reproduction stamps.

| PPR4 | 2012 Olympic Games 1948 | 40.00 | ☐ |

2013 Seahorses 1913 (19th September)

This fold-out pack commemorates the 150th Anniversary of the birth of Sir Edgar Bertram Mackennal, designer of the King George V Seahorses definitives. It includes pictures of his initial sketches and gives information about the printing process. Contains a block of four reproduction stamps.

| PPR5 | 2013 Seahorses 1913 | 12.50 | ☐ |

2014 Festival of Britain (25th March)

This pack, written by British Postal Museum & Archive curator Douglas Muir, looks at designer Abram Games's work, before focusing on his design of the original Festival logo and the special stamp celebrating the Festival. Contains a block of four reproduction stamps.

| PPR6 | 2014 Festival of Britain | 8.50 | ☐ |

Smilers for Kids

These special packs were issued in 2008 and 2009. They were designed specifically to appeal to children and, as well as 10 1st Class stamps, contain other 'fun' items such as notelets and cut-out face masks. A total of eight packs were produced.

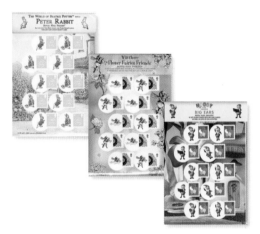

2008 Beatrix Potter (28th October)

This pack features Peter Rabbit and contains five 'baby announcement' cards, with places for adding a photograph. The stamp sheet consists of 10 'New Baby' 1st Class stamps, with two different images of Peter on adjoining labels.

| PPS1 | 2008 Beatrix Potter | 25.00 | ☐ |

2008 Flower Fairies Friends (28th October)

This pack features Almond Blossom and contains writing paper with matching envelopes and a cut-out Almond Blossom character. The stamp sheet consists of 10 1st Class 'sunflower' stamps, with an image of Almond Blossom on adjoining labels.

| PPS2 | 2008 Flower Fairies Friends | 25.00 | ☐ |

2008 Mr. Men and Little Miss (28th October)

This pack features Mr. Happy and contains a bookmark, a sheet of stickers and Mr. Happy's light-hearted tips for a happy life. The stamp sheet consists of 10 1st Class 'balloons' stamps, with five different images of Mr. Happy on adjoining labels.

| PPS3 | 2008 Mr. Men and Little Miss | 25.00 | ☐ |

2008 Noddy and Friends (28th October)

This pack features Noddy and contains colouring-in sheets, a spot-the-difference puzzle and a cut-out mask. The stamp sheet consists of 10 1st Class 'balloons' stamps, with 10 different images of Noddy on adjoining labels.

| PPS4 | 2008 Noddy and Friends | 25.00 | ☐ |

2009 Beatrix Potter (30th April)

This pack features Jeremy Fisher and contains colouring-in sheets, a spot-the-difference puzzle and a cut-out mask. The stamp sheet consists of 10 1st Class 'hello' stamps, with seven different images of Jeremy on adjoining labels.

| PPS5 | 2009 Beatrix Potter | 25.00 | ☐ |

2009 Flower Fairies Friends (30th April)

This pack features Wild Cherry and contains writing paper with matching envelopes and a cut-out Wild Cherry character. The stamp sheet consists of 10 1st Class 'sunflower' stamps, with two different images of Wild Cherry on adjoining labels.

| PPS6 | 2009 Flower Fairies Friends | 25.00 | ☐ |

2009 Mr. Men and Little Miss (30th April)

This pack features Little Miss Sunshine and contains a bookmark, a sheet of stickers and Little Miss Sunshine's light-hearted tips for a happy life. The stamp sheet consists of 10 1st Class 'balloons' stamps, with 10 different images of Little Miss Sunshine on adjoining labels.

| PPS7 | 2009 Mr. Men and Little Miss | 25.00 | ☐ |

2009 Noddy and Friends (30th April)

This pack features Big Ears and contains colouring-in sheets, a spot-the-difference puzzle and a cut-out mask. The stamp sheet consists of 10 1st Class 'balloons' stamps, with four different images of Big Ears on adjoining labels.

| PPS8 | 2009 Noddy and Friends | 25.00 | ☐ |

Year Packs and Year Books

Year Packs

Also known as Gift Packs or Collectors Packs, typically they contain all the commemorative stamps issued in a calendar year. Exceptions to this are packs issued between 1968 and 1971, the contents of which are detailed under the relevant listings.

Year Books

These are hardback books presented within a rigid outer sleeve. Each book contains every stamp issued in a calendar year. Since 1989, miniature sheets have also been included. Luxury, leather-bound editions are also available.

1967 Year Pack (27th November)

A complete set of the Commemorative stamps issued throughout the year; EFTA, Flora, Painters, Discovery, Chichester and Christmas. (Qty. sold 105,577)

| PPYP1 | 1967 Year Pack | 5.00 | ☐ |

1968 Year Pack - Blue (16th September)

Contains Commemorative stamps; 1967 Discovery, 1967 Christmas, 1968 Bridges, 1968 Anniversaries, 1968 Paintings. (Qty. sold 41,308)

Type a   Type b

PPYP2	1968 Year Pack - Blue	5.00	☐
a	Unicorn's leg not in line with scroll	8.00	☐
b	Unicorn's leg in line with scroll	5.00	☐

1968 Year Pack - Red (16th September)

A collection of three sets of Commemorative stamps from the year; Bridges, Anniversaries and Paintings - Christmas omitted. (Qty. sold 26,284; German Qty. sold 1,650)

| PPYP3 | 1968 Year Pack - Red | 5.00 | ☐ |
| g | German language pack | 75.00 | ☐ |

1969 Year Pack (15 September)

Contains Commemorative stamps; 1968 Christmas, 1969 Ships, 1969 Concorde, 1969 Anniversaries, 1969 Cathedrals, 1969 Investiture, 1969 Ghandi. (Qty. sold 63,890)

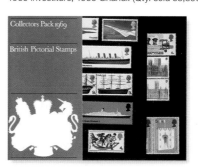

PPYP4	1969 Year Pack	18.00	☐
g	German insert card	12.00	☐
j	Japanese insert card	12.00	☐

1970 Year Pack (14th September)

Contains Commemorative stamps; 1969 Post Office Technology, 1969 Christmas, 1970 Rural Architecture, 1970 General Anniversaries, 1970 Literary Anniversaries, 1970 Commonwealth Games. (Qty. sold 54,768)

PPYP5	1970 Year Pack	19.00	☐
g	German insert card	12.00	☐
j	Japanese insert card	12.00	☐

1971 Year Pack (29th September)

Contains Commemorative stamps; 1970 Philympia, 1970 Christmas, 1971 Ulster Paintings, 1971 Literary Anniversaries, 1971 General Anniversaries, 1971 Universities. (Qty. sold 42,500)

PPYP6	1971 Year Pack	20.00	☐
g	German insert card	12.00	☐

1972 Year Pack (20th November)

A complete collection of stamps as found in the year's Commemorative Presentation Packs. Contains images and information about each set. (Qty. sold 33,380)

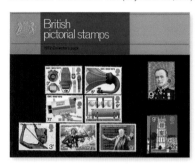

Type a

Type b

PPYP7	1972 Year Pack	20.00	☐
a	No flower between Unicorn's legs	20.00	☐
b	Flower between Unicorn's legs	20.00	☐
g	German insert card	12.00	☐

1973 Year Pack (28th November)

A complete collection of stamps as found in the year's Commemorative Presentation Packs. Contains images and information about each set. (Qty. sold 25,683)

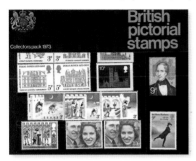

PPYP8	1973 Year Pack	16.00	☐
g	German insert card	9.00	☐

1974 Year Pack (27th November)

A complete collection of stamps as found in the year's Commemorative Presentation Packs. Contains images and information about each set. (Qty. sold 42,860)

PPYP9	1974 Year Pack	15.00	☐
g	German insert card	9.00	☐

1975 Year Pack (26th November)

A complete collection of stamps as found in the year's Commemorative Presentation Packs. Contains images and information about each set.

PPYP10	1975 Year Pack	8.00	☐

1976 Year Pack (24th November)

A complete collection of stamps as found in the year's Commemorative Presentation Packs. Contains images and information about each set.

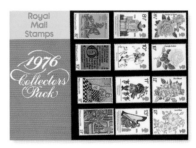

PPYP11	1976 Year Pack	8.00	☐

1977 Year Pack (23rd November)

A complete collection of stamps as found in the year's Commemorative Presentation Packs. Contains images and information about each set.

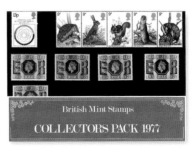

PPYP12	1977 Year Pack	7.00	☐

1978 Year Pack (22nd November)
A complete collection of stamps as found in the year's Commemorative Presentation Packs. Contains images and information about each set.

PPYP13 1978 Year Pack   7.00   ☐

1979 Year Pack (21st November)
A complete collection of stamps as found in the year's Commemorative Presentation Packs. Contains images and information about each set.

PPYP14 1979 Year Pack   7.00   ☐

1980 Year Pack (19th November)
A complete collection of stamps as found in the year's Commemorative Presentation Packs. Contains images and information about each set.

PPYP15 1980 Year Pack   7.00   ☐

1981 Year Pack (18th November)
A complete collection of stamps as found in the year's Commemorative Presentation Packs. Contains images and information about each set.

PPYP16 1981 Year Pack   9.00   ☐

1982 Year Pack (17th November)
A complete collection of stamps as found in the year's Commemorative Presentation Packs. Contains images and information about each set.

PPYP17 1982 Year Pack   12.00   ☐

1983 Year Pack (16th November)
A complete collection of stamps as found in the year's Commemorative Presentation Packs. Contains images and information about each set.

PPYP18 1983 Year Pack   12.00   ☐

1984 Year Pack (20th November)

A complete collection of stamps as found in the year's Commemorative Presentation Packs. Contains images and information about each set.

PPYP19 1984 Year Pack   15.00   ☐

1985 Year Pack (19th November)

A complete collection of stamps as found in the year's Commemorative Presentation Packs. Contains images and information about each set.

PPYP20 1985 Year Pack   15.00   ☐

1986 Year Pack (18th November)

A complete collection of stamps as found in the year's Commemorative Presentation Packs. Contains images and information about each set.

PPYP21 1986 Year Pack   15.00   ☐

1987 Year Pack (17th November)

A complete collection of stamps as found in the year's Commemorative Presentation Packs. Contains images and information about each set.

PPYP22 1987 Year Pack   15.00   ☐

1988 Year Pack (15th November)

A complete collection of stamps as found in the year's Commemorative Presentation Packs. Contains images and information about each set.

PPYP23 1988 Year Pack   15.00   ☐

1989 Year Pack (14th November)

A complete collection of stamps as found in the year's Commemorative Presentation Packs. Contains images and information about each set.

PPYP24 1989 Year Pack   15.00   ☐

1990 Year Pack (13th November)

A complete collection of stamps as found in the year's Commemorative Presentation Packs. Contains images and information about each set.

PPYP25 1990 Year Pack   15.00   ☐

1991 Year Pack (13th November)

A complete collection of stamps as found in the year's Commemorative Presentation Packs. Contains images and information about each set.

PPYP26 1991 Year Pack   16.00   ☐

1992 Year Pack (10th November)

A complete collection of stamps as found in the year's Commemorative Presentation Packs. Contains images and information about each set.

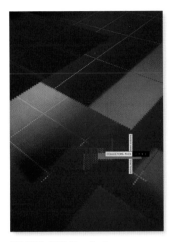

PPYP27 1992 Year Pack   16.00 ☐

1994 Year Pack (14th November)

A complete collection of stamps as found in the year's Commemorative Presentation Packs. Contains images and information about each set.

PPYP29 1994 Year Pack   24.00 ☐

1993 Year Pack (9th November)

A complete collection of stamps as found in the year's Commemorative Presentation Packs. Contains images and information about each set.

PPYP28 1993 Year Pack   16.00 ☐

1995 Year Pack (30th October)

A complete collection of stamps as found in the year's Commemorative Presentation Packs and Greetings Pack. Contains images and information about each set.

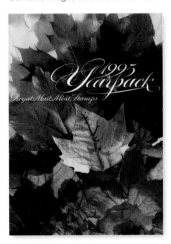

PPYP30 1995 Year Pack   24.00 ☐

1996 Year Pack (28th October)

A complete collection of stamps as found in the year's Commemorative Presentation Packs and Greetings pack. Contains images and information about each set.

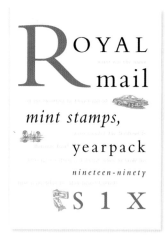

PPYP31 1996 Year Pack   28.00 ☐

1997 Year Pack (13th November)

A complete collection of stamps as found in the year's Commemorative Presentation Packs. Contains images and information about each set.

PPYP32 1997 Year Pack   28.00 ☐

1998 Year Pack (2nd November)

A complete collection of stamps as found in the year's Commemorative Presentation Packs. Contains images and information about each set.

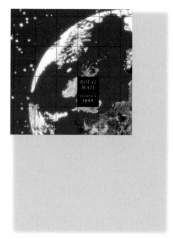

PPYP33 1998 Year Pack   32.00 ☐

1999 Year Pack (7th December)

A complete collection of stamps as found in the year's Commemorative Presentation Packs. Contains images and information about each set.

PPYP34 1999 Year Pack   45.00 ☐

2000 Year Pack (5th December)

A complete collection of stamps as found in the year's Commemorative Presentation Packs. Contains images and information about each set.

PPYP35 2000 Year Pack   50.00 ☐

2002 Year Pack (5th November)

A complete collection of stamps as found in the year's Commemorative Presentation Packs. Contains images and information about each set.

PPYP37 2002 Year Pack   65.00 ☐

2001 Year Pack (6th November)

A complete collection of stamps as found in the year's Commemorative Presentation Packs. Contains images and information about each set.

PPYP36 2001 Year Pack   55.00 ☐

2003 Year Pack (4th November)

A complete collection of stamps as found in the year's Commemorative Presentation Packs. Contains images and information about each set.

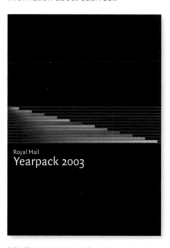

PPYP38 2003 Year Pack   75.00 ☐

2004 Year Pack (2nd November)

A complete collection of stamps as found in the year's Commemorative Presentation Packs. Contains images and information about each set.

PPYP39 2004 Year Pack   72.00 ☐

2005 Year Pack (2nd November)

A complete collection of stamps as found in the year's Commemorative Presentation Packs. Contains images and information about each set.

PPYP40 2005 Year Pack   72.00 ☐

2006 Year Pack (2nd November)

A complete collection of stamps as found in the year's Commemorative Presentation Packs. Contains images and information about each set.

PPYP41 2006 Year Pack   72.00 ☐

2007 Year Pack (8th November)

A complete collection of stamps as found in the year's Commemorative Presentation Packs. Contains images and information about each set.

PPYP42 2007 Year Pack   105.00 ☐

2008 Year Pack (6th November)

A complete collection of stamps as found in the year's Commemorative Presentation Packs. Contains images and information about each set.

PPYP43 2008 Year Pack   95.00 ☐

2009 Year Pack (3rd November)

A complete collection of stamps as found in the year's Commemorative Presentation Packs. Contains images and information about each set.

PPYP44 2009 Year Pack   98.00 ☐

2010 Year Pack (2nd November)

A complete collection of stamps as found in the year's Commemorative Presentation Packs. Contains images and information about each set.

PPYP45 2010 Year Pack   120.00 ☐

2011 Year Pack (8th November)

A complete collection of stamps as found in the year's Commemorative Presentation Packs. Contains images and information about each set.

PPYP46 2011 Year Pack   125.00 ☐

2012 Year Pack (6th November)

A complete collection of stamps as found in the year's Commemorative Presentation Packs. Contains images and information about each set.

PPYP47 2012 Year Pack   125.00 ☐

2013 Year Pack (5th November)

A complete collection of stamps as found in the year's Commemorative Presentation Packs. Contains images and information about each set.

PPYP48 2013 Year Pack   130.00 ☐

1984 Year Book (20th November)

Presented in a hardbound book with slip case are all the year's special stamp issues, alongside facts and images for each one.

PPYB1   1984 Year Book   60.00   ☐

1985 Year Book (19th November)

Presented in a hardbound book with slip case are all the year's special stamp issues, alongside facts and images for each one.

PPYB2   1985 Year Book   32.00   ☐

1986 Year Book (18th November)

Presented in a hardbound book with slip case are all the year's special stamp issues, alongside facts and images for each one.

PPYB3   1986 Year Book   32.00   ☐

1987 Year Book (17th November)

Presented in a hardbound book with slip case are all the year's special stamp issues, alongside facts and images for each one.

PPYB4   1987 Year Book   24.00   ☐

1988 Year Book (15th November)

Presented in a hardbound book with slip case are all the year's special stamp issues, alongside facts and images for each one.

PPYB5   1988 Year Book   24.00   ☐

Note: Some copies of this book contain a 13p stamp as part of the Christmas set, instead of a 14p stamp. The 13p stamp was never issued for general circulation and is therefore very scarce.

1989 Year Book (14th November)

Presented in a hardbound book with slip case are all the year's special stamp issues, alongside facts and images for each one.

PPYB6   1989 Year Book   24.00   ☐

1990 Year Book (13th November)

Presented in a hardbound book with slip case are all the year's special stamp issues, alongside facts and images for each one.

PPYB7   1990 Year Book   24.00   ☐

1991 Year Book (12th November)

Presented in a hardbound book with slip case are all the year's special stamp issues, alongside facts and images for each one.

PPYB8   1991 Year Book   24.00   ☐

1992 Year Book (11th November)

Presented in a hardbound book with slip case are all the year's special stamp issues, alongside facts and images for each one.

PPYB9   1992 Year Book   25.00   ☐

1993 Year Book (9th November)

Presented in a hardbound book with slip case are all the year's special stamp issues, alongside facts and images for each one.

PPYB10 1993 Year Book   26.00   ☐

1994 Year Book (1st November)

Presented in a hardbound book with slip case are all the year's special stamp issues, alongside facts and images for each one.

PPYB11 1994 Year Book   26.00   ☐

1995 Year Book (30th October)

Presented in a hardbound book with slip case are all the year's special stamp issues, alongside facts and images for each one.

PPYB12 1995 Year Book   25.00   ☐

1996 Year Book (28th October)

Presented in a hardbound book with slip case are all the year's special stamp issues, alongside facts and images for each one.

PPYB13 1996 Year Book   27.50 ☐

1997 Year Book (13th November)

Presented in a hardbound book with slip case are all the year's special stamp issues, alongside facts and images for each one.

PPYB14 1997 Year Book   26.00 ☐

1998 Year Book (2nd November)

Presented in a hardbound book with slip case are all the year's special stamp issues, alongside facts and images for each one.

PPYB15 1998 Year Book   30.00 ☐

1999 Year Book (7th December)

Presented in a hardbound book with slip case are all the year's special stamp issues, alongside facts and images for each one.

PPYB16 1999 Year Book   45.00 ☐

2000 Year Book (7th November)

Presented in a hardbound book with slip case are all the year's special stamp issues, alongside facts and images for each one.

PPYB17 2000 Year Book   52.00 ☐

2001 Year Book (6th November)

Presented in a hardbound book with slip case are all the year's special stamp issues, alongside facts and images for each one.

FLOWERLOVERSBUT
ALSOANATIONOFST
AMPCOLLECTORSPI
GEONFANCIERSAMA
TEURCARPENTERSC
OUPONSNIPPERSDA
RTSPLAYERSCROSS
WORDPUZZLEFANS
2001 ROYAL MAIL SPECIAL STAMPS 18

PPYB18 2001 Year Book   54.00 ☐

2002 Year Book (5th November)

Presented in a hardbound book with slip case are all the year's special stamp issues, alongside facts and images for each one.

PPYB19 2002 Year Book   56.00   ☐

2003 Year Book (4th November)

Presented in a hardbound book with slip case are all the year's special stamp issues, alongside facts and images for each one.

PPYB20 2003 Year Book   68.00   ☐

2004 Year Book (2nd November)

Presented in a hardbound book with slip case are all the year's special stamp issues, alongside facts and images for each one.

PPYB21 2004 Year Book   56.00   ☐

2005 Year Book (2nd November)

Presented in a hardbound book with slip case are all the year's special stamp issues, alongside facts and images for each one.

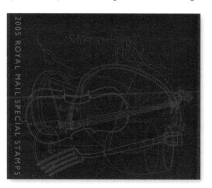

PPYB22 2005 Year Book   68.00   ☐

2006 Year Book (2nd November)

2006 saw a change in Year Book presentation, from being in an outer slip case to a box. The hardbound book contains all the year's special stamp issues, alongside facts and images for each one.

A BOXFUL OF ROYAL MAIL STAMPS FOR YOU TO ENJOY In this book you'll find everything you'll ever need to know about the great heroes of the past alongside the movers and shapers who're creating the dynamic world of today. It's a real treasure trove of ideas and inspiration – go back with us into the Ice Age, join in the fun with The Queen's 80th birthday and bop till you drop with Britain's funkiest, most danceable sounds. There are over ten exclusive interviews with celebrities like Ricky Gervais, David Dimbleby and Private Johnson Beharry the first man in the 21st century to receive the Victoria Cross. And it doesn't stop there. This book also includes all twelve complete sets of Royal Mail Special Stamps issued during the course of the year together with full philatelic information on each and every issue. They are presented here in mint condition and ready for you to place in their designated position alongside short feature articles on how they were created by Britain's world-leading stamp designers. This highly collectible, 64-page all-colour book is packed with photographs of the famous and the obscure – it's the definitive story behind an entire year of birthdays, anniversaries and other celebrations. Now that they've gone, ISSUE 23 2006 is perfect for recalling the last twelve months.

PPYB23 2006 Year Book   75.00   ☐

2007 Year Book (8th November)

Presented in a box, this hardbound book contains all the year's special stamp issues, alongside facts and images for each one.

PPYB24 2007 Year Book   95.00   ☐

2008 Year Book (6th November)

Presented in a box, this hardbound book contains all the year's special stamp issues, alongside facts and images for each one.

PPYB25 2008 Year Book   90.00 ☐

2009 Year Book (3rd November)

Presented in a box, this hardbound book contains all the year's special stamp issues, alongside facts and images for each one.

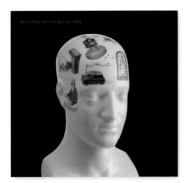

PPYB26 2009 Year Book   92.00 ☐

2010 Year Book (2nd November)

Presented in a box, this hardbound book contains all the year's special stamp issues, alongside facts and images for each one.

PPYB27 2010 Year Book   120.00 ☐

2011 Year Book (8th November)

Presented in a box, this hardbound book contains all the year's special stamp issues, alongside facts and images for each one.

PPYB28 2011 Year Book   130.00 ☐

2012 Year Book (6th November)

Presented in a box, this hardbound book contains all the year's special stamp issues, alongside facts and images for each one.

PPYB29 2012 Year Book   195.00 ☐

2013 Year Book (5th November)

Presented in a box, this hardbound book contains all the year's special stamp issues, alongside facts and images for each one.

PPYB30 2013 Year Book   135.00 ☐

Souvenir and Special Edition Packs

This section contains a wide variety of packs varying in style, content and size. They were all produced by Royal Mail and some were distributed by third parties.

The packs in this section have not been allocated a catalogue number as there might be others uncovered that, when interspersed chronologically, would void a sequential numbering system.

1969 British Ships (Cunard) (15th January)

This issue is a tribute to British shipbuilders and seamen and describes six famous British ships, as illustrated on the stamps. What differentiates this pack from PP24 is that, because the sailing of the QE2 was delayed, the incorrect departure date previously printed inside was replaced with "early in 1969" (original printing reads "to New York on 17th January 1969"). This pack was sold exclusively on the QE2.

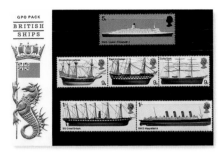

Normal	Cunard
and she sailed on her maiden voyage to New York on 17th January 1969.	and she sails on her maiden voyage early in 1969.

1969 British Ships (Cunard) 24.00 ☐

1971 Scandinavia (15th February)

Marking the advent of decimalisation, the first set of decimal definitive stamps was brought together in this Souvenir pack and promoted in all three Scandinavian countries during a BPO Tour. Inside the pack are details of the stamps and Tour dates. A separate insert card gives translations into the language of each country visited.

1971 Scandinavia 50.00 ☐
 Multi-language insert card 350.00 ☐
 (Danish, Norwegian, Swedish)

1971 Heinz (13th October)

This Special Edition pack was used by Heinz to promote their soup and lists their extensive range of flavours. For sending in eight different soup labels, you received this pack and the enclosed six 2½p stamps from the Christmas issue.

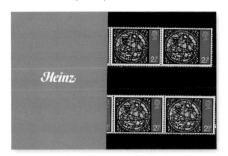

1971 Heinz 32.00 ☐

1971 NABA 2 Wallets (3rd November)

Small Format Special Packs. One wallet contains Definitives up to £1 and the other 'To Pay' Labels.

Wallet front

Wallet inside
(Definitives)

Wallet inside
(To Pay)

1971 NABA 2 Wallets 80.00 ☐

1972 Belgica (24th June)

This Souvenir pack was issued to commemorate the BPO's exhibit at Belgica '72, for which the theme was religious architecture and art. Written in English, French and German, the pack contains stamp issues 1971 Christmas and 1972 Village Churches, plus 10 pages of information, images and other stamp designs. (Qty. sold 20,672)

1972 Belgica   10.00   ☐

1972 Royal Silver Wedding Souvenir

(20th November)

This Souvenir pack was issued as a memento of the occasion of The Queen's 25th Wedding Anniversary. Fully illustrated, it contains the 1972 Silver Wedding stamp issue, plus 12 pages of information, photos and other stamp designs, all relating to the Royal Wedding and the Royal Family. (Qty. sold 65,425)

1972 Royal Silver Wedding Souvenir (printed no.46)   4.00   ☐

1973 County Cricket Souvenir (16th May)

This pack was issued as a souvenir of the Centenary of County Cricket. Fully illustrated, it contains the 1973 County Cricket stamp issue, plus 24 pages of photos and information about some of the best players in England, along with the history of this peculiarly English activity. (Qty. sold 28,576)

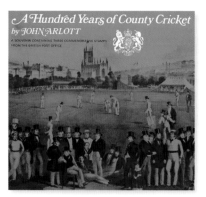

1973 County Cricket Souvenir   6.00   ☐

1973 Palace of Westminster Souvenir

(12th September)

Fully illustrated, this Souvenir pack contains the 1973 Commonwealth Parliamentary Conference stamp issue, plus 24 pages of diagrams, photos and information about the history of the Palace of Westminster, including Westminster Hall and the Houses of Parliament. (Qty. sold 17,920)

1973 Palace of Westminster Souvenir (printed no.55)   6.00   ☐

1974 Churchill Souvenir (9th October)

This Special Edition pack was issued to mark the Centenary of the birth of Winston Churchill. Fully illustrated, it has the 1974 Churchill stamp issue in a plastic 'bubble' on the cover, plus six pages of photos and information about his life, from commission into the 4th Hussars, in 1895, to his retirement from office in 1955.

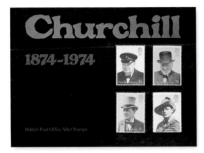

| 1974 Churchill Souvenir | 5.00 | ☐ |

1975 Railways Souvenir (13th August)

Marking the 150th Anniversary of the first public steam railway, this Special Edition pack contains the 1975 Railways stamp issue in a plastic 'bubble' on the cover, plus 20 pages of illustrations, photos and information about the development of rail travel, from Stephenson's Locomotion to modern high-speed trains.

| 1975 Railways Souvenir (printed no.73) | 5.00 | ☐ |

1977 Silver Jubilee Souvenir (11th May)

This Souvenir pack was issued to commemorate The Silver Jubilee of The Queen's Accession to the throne. Fully illustrated, the 1977 Silver Jubilee stamp issue is enclosed on the cover, and it contains 16 pages of photos and information about The Queen's Royal duties and the Royal Family.

| 1977 Silver Jubilee Souvenir | 4.00 | ☐ |

1978 25th Anniversary of Coronation Souvenir (31st May)

This Souvenir pack was issued to commemorate the 25th Anniversary of The Queen's Coronation. Fully illustrated, the 1978 Coronation stamp issue is enclosed on the cover, and it contains 16 pages of photos and information about the ceremony and accompanying regalia.

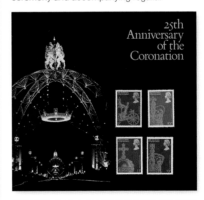

| 1978 25th Anniversary of Coronation Souvenir | 4.00 | ☐ |

1981 The Royal Wedding Souvenir (22nd July)

This Souvenir pack was issued to commemorate The Royal Wedding of HRH The Prince of Wales and Lady Diana Spencer, at St Paul's Cathedral, London, on 29th July 1981. Fully illustrated, it contains the 1981 Royal Wedding stamp issue, plus 12 pages of photos and information about previous Royal Weddings.

| 1981 The Royal Wedding Souvenir | 3.00 | ☐ |

1981 The Royal Wedding - Japanese (22nd July)

Produced by a British overseas agent for the 1981 Toyko Philatelic Show, this Japanese Souvenir pack contains the 1981 Royal Wedding stamps. The main text is in Japanese, with 'British Post Office' written in English on the reverse. It is believed that this pack was not proofread by the Post Office before being sold at the Show. When the packs were sent to the Philatelic Bureau, for selling to British collectors, it was claimed that the Japanese text suggested that Prince Charles had to stand on a box to be taller than Diana. Subsequently, the pack was reprinted with this information removed.

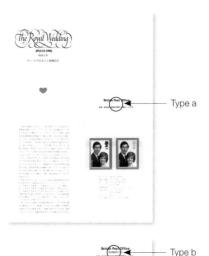

Type a

Type b

1981 The Royal Wedding - Japanese	6.00	☐
a Two lines of writing on reverse	6.00	☐
b Three lines of writing on reverse	6.00	☐

1981 Royal Wedding - Cadbury Typhoo (22nd July)

To commemorate the wedding of HRH The Prince of Wales and Lady Diana Spencer, this presentation pack was published by the Post Office for Cadbury Typhoo Limited and included a booklet on Royal commemorative stamps.

| 1981 Royal Wedding - Cadbury Typhoo | 5.00 | ☐ |

1982 IT Electronic Post (22nd July)

Supported by government and industry, Royal Mail designated 1982 as their year of Information Technology. Inside, the pack describes the use of space-age technology to achieve a formidable new service to handle bulk mailing. Contains the 1982 Information Technology stamp issue.

Pack front

| 1982 IT Electronic Post | 180.00 | ☐ |

1984 Royal Mail Souvenir (31st July)

Issued to mark the 200th Anniversary of the inauguration of the 'Bristol, Bath, London' Mail. Fully illustrated, it contains the 1984 Royal Mail stamp issue, plus 24 pages of information showing many original documents and paintings, and the story of how the Royal Mail was created.

| 1984 Royal Mail Souvenir | 7.00 | ☐ |

1985 British Films Souvenir (8th October)

The British Film Year, from April 1985 to March 1986, was organised by film distributors and exhibitors to reverse the dramatic decline in cinema attendance. Fully illustrated, this Souvenir pack contains the 1985 British Film Year stamp issue, plus 24 pages of stills from some of the most popular films, along with the history of British film-making.

1985 British Films Souvenir	7.00 ☐

1985 Christmas 50 x 12p (19th November)

This Special Edition pack was used to promote an offer of six free postcards, featuring popular works of art from The National Gallery. Inside are details of how to apply for the offer using the attached coupon. Contains 50 x 12p stamps which are overlaid with metallic print stars.

1985 Christmas 50 x 12p	20.00 ☐

1986 Queen's Birthday Souvenir (21st April)

Issued in celebration of The Queen's 60th birthday, this fully illustrated Souvenir pack contains the 1986 60th Birthday stamp issue, plus 32 pages of photos and information giving an insight into her family and 'work' life.

1986 Queen's Birthday Souvenir	9.00 ☐

1986 Christmas 36 x 13p (18th November)

This Special Edition pack contains 36 x 13p stamps from the 1986 Christmas issue. Inside tells the legend of The Glastonbury Thorn which is illustrated on the stamps.

1986 Christmas 36 x 13p	9.00 ☐

Also exists with a barcode sticker fixed to the back, for sales through non-Post Office outlets.

1987 Christmas 36 x 13p (17th November)

This Special Edition pack contains 36 x 13p stamps from the 1987 Christmas issue. Inside is a guide to postage rates and last posting dates.

1987 Christmas 36 x 13p	9.00 ☐

1988 Australian Bicentenary Souvenir (21st June)

This Souvenir pack was issued to mark the Bicentenary of British settlement in Australia. It contains a joint issue of eight stamps (four British and four Australian) plus 40 pages of photos, illustrations and information about the close bond between Britain and Australia.

1988 Australian Bicentenary Souvenir	12.00 ☐

1990 Penny Black Anniversary Book (10th January)

To celebrate the 150th Anniversary of the Penny Black, this Souvenir captures the real significance of the stamp. It tells the story of the design and printing of the Penny Black and various other stamps that have led to the Anniversary issue, including the Seahorses stamps and the Machin definitives. Contains five stamps, a miniature sheet and a reproduction of an original Mulready envelope.

1990 Penny Black Anniversary Book	12.00	☐

1994 Channel Tunnel - joint pack (3rd May)

A joint issue between Royal Mail and La Poste, this Special Edition pack gives a brief history of the Channel Tunnel. Written in English and French, it contains a joint issue of eight stamps (four British and four French).

1994 Channel Tunnel - joint pack	20.00	☐

1995 National Trust. 1st Class stamps (11th April)

A blister pack of 10 1st Class stamps, produced to mark the Centenary of The National Trust.

1995 National Trust. 1st Class stamps	11.00	☐

1995 National Trust. 2nd Class stamps (11th April)

A blister pack of 10 2nd Class stamps, produced to mark the Centenary of The National Trust.

1995 National Trust. 2nd Class stamps	10.00	☐

1996 M&S. 1st Class stamps

A blister pack of 10 1st Class stamps, sold through Marks & Spencer stores.

1996 M&S. 1st Class stamps	15.00	☐

1996 M&S. 2nd Class stamps

A blister pack of 10 2nd Class stamps, sold through Marks & Spencer stores.

1996 M&S. 2nd Class stamps	14.00	☐

1996 Capex Souvenir (16th April)

A Souvenir of Capex '96 Stamp Exhibition which took place in Toronto, Canada, 8th-16th June 1996. The pack contains HRH Queen Elizabeth's 60th birthday label stamp pane.

1996 Capex Souvenir   7.00   ☐

1996 China Souvenir (16th April)

A Souvenir of China '96 Stamp Exhibition which took place in Bejing on 18th-24th May 1996. Written in English and Chinese, the pack contains HRH Queen Elizabeth's 60th birthday label stamp pane.

1996 China Souvenir   7.00   ☐

1997 Hong Kong Souvenir (12th February)

A Souvenir of Hong Kong '97 Stamp Exhibition. Written in English and Chinese, the pack contains HRH Queen Elizabeth's 60th birthday label stamp pane.

1997 Hong Kong Souvenir   10.00   ☐

1997 Golden Wedding Souvenir (13th November)

A Souvenir to commemorate the Golden Wedding Anniversary of The Queen and Prince Philip. This book contains a 1st Class stamp on the cover, 1997 All The Queen's Horses stamps, 1997 Golden Wedding stamps featuring a specially-commissioned portrait by Lord Snowdon, plus eight pages of commemorative photos and eight tear-out stamp cards.

1997 Golden Wedding Souvenir   24.00   ☐

2000 Stamp Show - Millennium Timekeeper
(22nd May)

This pack is a Premium Show Pass to The Stamp Show 2000, allowing admission on the Premium Show Day and for the remainder of the event. Contains a complementary, overprinted, Millennium Timekeeper Miniature Sheet.

2000 Stamp Show - Millennium Timekeeper   20.00   ☐

2000 Stamp Show - Matthews Palette (23rd May)

To commemorate The Stamp Show 2000, this Exhibition Souvenir Pack contains two Matthews Palette Miniature Sheets; one mint and one FDI cancelled.

2000 Stamp Show - Matthews Palette   55.00   ☐

2000 Stamp Show - Prestige Books (23rd May)

Issued for The Stamp Show 2000, this high quality pack contains three prestige booklets and a special, cancelled, Miniature Sheet.

2000 Stamp Show - Prestige Books	95.00	☐

2003 Coronation £10 Postal Order (2nd July)

Produced to commemorate the 50th Anniversary of The Queen's Coronation, this pack gives a brief history of Postal Orders and contains a special edition £10 Order, cancelled by the Windsor post office. (Qty. issued 50,000)

2003 Coronation £10 Postal Order	90.00	☐

2004 Classic Locomotives - M/S pack

(13th January)

Commemorating the 200th Anniversary of the first journey on rails by a steam locomotive, in February 1804. Contains a miniature sheet of six 1st Class stamps rather than six single stamps as in the standard pack (PP325).

2004 Classic Locomotives - M/S pack	12.00	☐

2004 Entente Cordiale - joint pack (6th April)

In this pack, Royal Mail and La Poste joined forces to celebrate the Centenary of the Entente Cordiale, or 'friendly understanding' between France and Great Britain. Written in English and French, it contains a joint issue of eight stamps (four British and four French).

2004 Entente Cordiale - joint pack	15.00	☐

2005 World Heritage - joint pack (21st April)

This Souvenir pack is an Australia-UK joint issue which features four World Heritage Areas from each nation including the monolithic Uluru, in the sandy plains of central Australia; the grey stones of Hadrian's Wall in England; the eucalyptic forest of the Blue Mountains in New South Wales and the palatial Blenheim Palace in Oxfordshire. Contains a joint issue of 16 stamps (eight British and eight Australian).

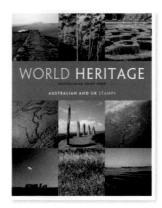

2005 World Heritage - joint pack	35.00	☐

2008 Lest We Forget - M/S Collection (11th November)

This Special Edition pack, containing three Miniature Sheets, folds out into a Remembrance Cross featuring the role of the postal service during the First World War, at home and on the Front. In addition to the Miniature Sheets, the pack also contains a replica embroidered postcard - a popular item sent home from the trenches.

2008 Lest We Forget - M/S Collection   35.00 ☐

2009 Brilliant Britain - M/S Collection (6th March)

This gorgeous pack contains all four Miniature Sheets from the popular 'Celebrating' series. It folds out to reveal a Royal Mail compass and map of the Britsh Isles.

2009 Brilliant Britain - M/S Collection   29.00 ☐

2009 Military Uniforms Collection (17th September)

Containing the Special Stamps from all three parts of the Military Uniforms series, this fascinating pack also includes a high quality replica of a Post Office Rifles cap badge.

2009 Military Uniforms Collection   29.00 ☐

2011 Harry Potter Heroes & Villains (30th November)

Issued to celebrate the DVD launch of the final adventure in the Harry Potter film series, this Special pack was released to collectors only, without publicity. Contains a double-sided poster of Dumbledore and Lord Voldemort, plus a block of 10 1st Class stamps (five x Dumbledore, five x Lord Voldemort) which were originally issued in the 2011 Magical Realms pack.

2011 Harry Potter Heroes & Villains   12.00 ☐

Private Packs

A Private Pack, whilst containing Royal Mail stamps, is produced and published by a third party. This section lists those considered the most noteworthy and significant.

Packs in this section have not been allocated catalogue numbers due to the likelihood of additional packs being included in future editions.

Post Office Missed
Also known as POM packs, this interesting series of 16 presentation packs was created for stamp issues that the Post Office 'Missed' out of pack production e.g the 1967 Christmas stamps. Although the stamp issues range from the 1937 Coronation of King George VI to the 1977 Silver Jubilee 9p, the packs were all published in the 1960s and 1970s.

Aberdeen
Produced by Aberdeen Publicity Department, this series of packs spans six years, commencing with the 1976 Roses issue.

Airline
Throughout 1977 and 1978, several airlines published their own presentation packs, sometimes using their own design and sometimes by overprinting an existing Royal Mail pack.

Bournemouth
From 1975 to 1984, The Bournemouth & District Philatelic Society produced their own series of 10 presentation packs, printed in limited editions of 1,000 each.

Norwich
These packs were produced by Dereham Stamp Centre to commemorate special occasions, such as The Queen Mother's 80th birthday and her connections with Norfolk.

1937 Coronation (13th May)

Containing a 1937 stamp issued to mark the Coronation of King George VI and Queen Elizabeth at Westminster Abbey on 12th May 1937, this pack contains a little information about Albert's life before his accession. (Qty. issued 2,000)

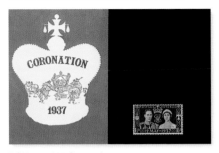

POM   1937 Coronation   13.50   ☐

1951 Festival of Britain (3rd May)

This scarce pack commemorates the Festival of Britain, held 100 years after the Great Exhibition of 1851, and contains information about the planning of this five-month event. (Qty. issued 2,000)

POM   1951 Festival of Britain   18.00   ☐

1965 Salvation Army Centenary (9th August)

Commemorating the Centenary of the Salvation Army, this pack tells the story of its founding by William Booth, the autocratic system that was adopted for governing the Salvationists, and their work to help the deprived. (Qty. issued 2,000)

POM   1965 Salvation Army Centenary   24.00   ☐

1965 Commonwealth Arts Festival (1st September)

This pack contains information about the Trinidad Carnival Dancers, who participated in the Festival, and of the cultural traditions of Canadian Folk Dancers. (Qty. issued 2,000)

POM   1965 Commonwealth Arts Festival   16.50   ☐

1965 Centenary of Joseph Lister's Introduction of Antiseptic Surgery (1st September)

To commemorate this important Anniversary, the pack tells the story of Lister's research and work on inflammation, and the subsequent influence of Louis Pasteur's discovery earlier in the same year. (Qty. issued 2,000)

POM   1965 Centenary of Joseph Lister's
Introduction of Antiseptic Surgery   16.50   ☐

1965 United Nations (25th October)

Issued to mark the 20th Anniversary of the Signing of the United Nations Charter, this pack contains information about the Security Council, General Assembly and other more specialised agencies which, together, make up the UN. (Qty. issued 2,000)

POM   1965 United Nations   13.00   ☐

1965 I.T.U. (15th November)

Issued to mark the Centenary of the International Telegraph Union, this pack tells of the 1932 meeting in Madrid which codified and combined two previous conventions and renamed 'Telegraph' to 'Telecommunications'. (Qty. issued 2,000)

| POM | 1965 I.T.U. | 13.00 | ☐ |

1966 Pictorial Issue (2nd May)

This pack celebrates the beauty of some typical landscapes found in England, Northern Ireland, Wales and Scotland, and discusses the views illustrated on the stamps. (Qty. issued 2,000)

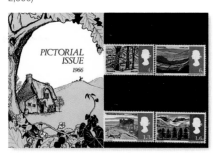

| POM | 1966 Pictorial Issue | 13.00 | ☐ |

1966 England's World Cup Victory (18th August)

To commemorate the victory of the England football team over West Germany on 30th July, this pack contains an overprinted version ("England Winners") of the 4d stamp issued a few months earlier. (Qty. issued 2,000)

| POM | 1966 England's World Cup Victory | 13.50 | ☐ |

1967 Chichester's World Voyage (24th July)

In recognition of Sir Francis Chichester's solo circumnavigation of the world by sail, this pack commemorates his remarkable achievement with the story of the voyage that culminated in his knighthood on 7th July 1967. (Qty. issued 2,000)

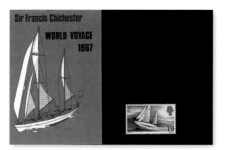

| POM | 1967 Chichester's World Voyage | 9.00 | ☐ |

1967 Christmas (27th November)

This pack features religious interpretations in art and discusses paintings by Murillo and Louis Le Nain, which provided inspiration for the designs of two of the enclosed stamps. (Qty. issued 2,000)

| POM | 1967 Christmas | 9.00 | ☐ |

1969 Gandhi Centenary Year (13th August)

Commemorating the Centenary of the birth of Mohandas Karamchand Gandhi, this pack tells the story of his career, imprisonment and anti-violence teachings, which led to his assassination in 1947. (Qty. issued 2,000)

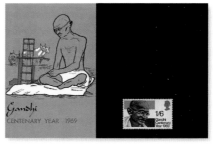

| POM | 1969 Gandhi Centenary Year | 9.00 | ☐ |

1975 Health and Handicap Charities (22nd January)

Marking the issue in Britain of the first Charity stamp, this pack describes how proceeds would be accrued from sales of the enclosed special stamp. (Qty. issued 2,000)

POM   1975 Health and Handicap Charities   8.00   ☐

1976 10p Booklet Pane (January) (10th January)

This pack tells the story of Arnold Machin's definitive stamp design and how it was incorporated. (Qty. issued 2,000)

POM   1976 10p Booklet Pane (January)   8.00   ☐

1976 10p Booklet Pane (March) (10th March)

This pack tells the story of Arnold Machin's definitive stamp design and how it was incorporated. (Qty. issued 2,000)

POM   1976 10p Booklet Pane (March)   8.00   ☐

1977 Silver Jubilee 9p (15th June)

The Silver Jubilee of The Queen's Accession to the throne is commemorated in this pack, which was the last of its type.
The Silver Jubilee 9p stamp was a subsequent issue to the four original stamps, but the Post Office didn't produce a pack for it. (Qty. issued 2,000)

POM   1977 Silver Jubilee 9p   8.00   ☐

1976 Roses (30th June)

Marking the Centenary of the Royal National Rose Society, this pack features a hybrid tea rose, a shrub rose, a briar and 'Elizabeth of Glamis', a floribunda named after the Queen Mother who was patron of the society. (Qty. issued 1,000)

Aberdeen 1976 Roses   100.00 ☐

1977 Silver Jubilee (11th May)

This pack was issued by the Aberdeen Publicity Department to commemorate the Queen's Silver Jubilee visit to Aberdeen. It includes interesting photographs from the visit and the Royal party's hectic programme. (Qty. issued 2,000)

Aberdeen 1977 Silver Jubilee   24.00 ☐

1978 Coronation Anniversary (31st May)

Commemorating the 25th Anniversary of the Coronation, this pack includes several interesting photos taken around Aberdeen during Coronation day.

Aberdeen 1978 Coronation Anniversary   8.00 ☐

1979 International Year of the Child (11th July)

This pack includes the Declaration of the Rights of the Child, which was laid down in 1959, and contains information about Aberdeen's 'Youth Spectacular' event, held to celebrate the International Year of the Child.

Aberdeen 1979 International Year of the Child   15.00 ☐

1980 Queen Mother (4th August)

To commemorate the Queen Mother's 80th birthday, this pack contains photographs and information about her love of Scotland and patronage of the National Trust there.

Aberdeen 1980 Queen Mother   16.00 ☐

1981 National Trust (24th June)

Marking the Golden Jubilee of the National Trust for Scotland, this pack features photos and descriptions of six Houses and Castles in Aberdeen, Deeside and Donside.

Aberdeen 1981 National Trust   15.00 ☐

1981 National Trust

Produced on the 50th Anniv[ersary of the]
Scotland, this pack tells the [...]
being the best-known Natio[nal...]
Dorset. (Qty. issued 1,000)

Bournemouth 1981 National [...]

1982 Maritime Histor[y]

This pack is full of informatio[n...]
regular steamship service to [...]
was started there. (Qty. issue[d...])

Bournemouth 1982 Maritime [...]

1983 Pleasure Garde[ns]

This pack was produced for th[e...]
which also marked the Bicent[...]
Brown, the landscape garden[er...]

Bournemouth 1983 Pleasure [...]

1977 Jubilee - Caledonian (11th May)

This pack was produced by British Caledonian Airways and
presented to First Class passengers on Jubilee Day. It is an
overprint of the 1977 Silver Jubilee Commemorative Pack.

Airline 1977 Jubilee - Caledonian   18.00   ☐

1977 Jubilee - Golden Lion Charity (11th May)

This pack is identical to the 'Caledonian' pack apart from an
additional overprint of the Goldon Lion Children's Charity logo.

Airline 1977 Jubilee - Golden Lion Charity   24.00   ☐

1978 Energy - Dan Air (25th January)

Produced to advertise Dan Air's Oil Support services, this is an
overprint of the 1978 Energy Commemorative Pack.

Airline 1978 Energy - Dan Air   24.00   ☐

1978 Energy - Dan Air (blue) (25th January)

This is the Airline's own presentation pack giving details of their
Oil Support services.

Airline 1978 Energy - Dan Air (blue)   25.00   ☐

1978 Historic Buildings (1st March)

This pack was issued by Air Anglia to mark the introduction
of the Fokker F.28 Fellowship into full time service on their
jet routings. The pack contains a stamp of Holyroodhouse,
Edinburgh, and a French stamp of Pont-Nuef, Paris.

Airline 1978 Historic Buildings   25.00   ☐

1978 25th Anniversary of the Coronation
(31st May)

BAF issued this pack to commemorate the inauguration of their
scheduled air services between Manchester and Rotterdam on
1st June 1978. It is an overprint of the 1978 Anniversary of the
Coronation Commemorative Pack.

Airline 1978 25th Anniversary of the Coronation 19.00   ☐

1975 Public Railways (2...

This pack celebrates the 150th ...
of the public steam passenger t...
which first ran on the Stockton t...
issued 1,000)

Bournemouth 1975 Public Railw...

1976 Telephone Centen...

Commemorating the Centenary ...
by Alexander Graham Bell on 10t...
the development of national phon...
country. (Qty. issued 1,000)

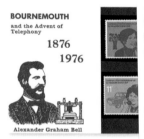

Bournemouth 1976 Telephone C...

1977 Silver Jubilee (24th S...

Commemorating the Silver Jubilee...
this pack also celebrates Bournem...
Anniversary, telling the history of t...
(Qty. issued 1,000)

Bournemouth 1977 Silver Jubilee...

1977 Scottish Wildlife Trust (green) (5th October)

Issued by the Scottish Wildlife Trust, this pack was designed to make children and adults more aware of the nation's wildlife heritage, and the need to protect it.

Private 1977 Scottish Wildlife Trust (green) 12.00 ☐

1978 Horses. Shire Horse Society (5th July)

This adapted presentation pack was produced exclusively for the Shire Horse Society, in its Centenary year. 1978 was also designated 'Year of the Horse' in the Chinese calendar and the pack contains both British and Hong Kong stamps.

Private 1978 Horses. Shire Horse Society 40.00 ☐

1978 Horses. Sawyer's Hall (5th July)

This presentation pack is a Limited Edition that was specially produced to commemorate the Sawyer's Hall Riding Establishment in Brentwood, Essex. (Qty. issued 500)

Private 1978 Horses. Sawyer's Hall 25.00 ☐

1978 Horses. Ingatestone & Blackmore (5th July)

This presentation pack is a Limited Edition that was specially produced to commemorate the Ingatestone & Blackmore Riding Club's Open Novice Jumping Show. (Qty. issued 500)

Private 1978 Horses. Ingatestone & Blackmore 25.00 ☐

1978 Horses. The Harlow Show (5th July)

This presentation pack is a Limited Edition that was specially produced to commemorate The Harlow Show of August 1978. (Qty. issued 1,000)

Private 1978 Horses. The Harlow Show 17.50 ☐

1978 Horses. Craen Riding Centre (5th July)

This presentation pack is a Limited Edition that was specially produced to commemorate the Craen Riding Centre, Welshpool. Craen is a small, working, hill farm located in mid-Wales. (Qty. issued 500)

Private 1978 Horses. Craen Riding Centre 25.00 ☐

1978 Horses. Nashes Stud Farm (5th July)

This presentation pack is a Limited Edition that was specially produced to commemorate Nashes Shetland Pony Stud Farm, Uckfield, Sussex. (Qty. issued 500)

| Private | 1978 Horses. Nashes Stud Farm | 25.00 | ☐ |

1978 Cwmfforrest Riding Centre (5th July)

This presentation pack is a Limited Edition that was specially produced to commemorate the Cwmfforest Riding Centre, a traditional hill farm set in the Black Mountains of Wales. (Qty. issued 500)

| Private | 1978 Horses. Cwmfforrest Riding Centre | 25.00 | ☐ |

1978 Indianapolis (21st September)

This pack was specially produced to be sold at the 92nd Annual APS Convention, held in Indianapolis 21st-24th September 1978. Contains both the Cycling and Horses stamp issues.

| Private | 1978 Indianapolis | 7.00 | ☐ |

1979 Dogs. The Harlow Show (7th February)

This pack is a Limited Edition that was specially produced to commemorate the Dog Show held during The Harlow Show of August 1979. (Qty. issued 500)

| Private | 1979 Dogs. The Harlow Show | 16.00 | ☐ |

1979 Dogs. Daily Mail Ideal Home (6th March)

This pack was specially produced as a Souvenir of the 1979 Daily Mail Ideal Home Exhibition, held at Earls Court, London.

| Private | 1979 Dogs. Daily Mail Ideal Home | 15.00 | ☐ |

1979 Scottish Wildlife Trust Flowers (21st March)

Issued by the Scottish Wildlife Trust, this pack was designed to make children and adults more aware of the nation's wildlife heritage, and the need to protect it.

| Private | 1979 Scottish Wildlife Trust Flowers | 15.00 | ☐ |

1979 Tunbridge Wells Stamp Fair Flowers
(21st March)

This pack was specially commisioned to commemorate the South of England Spring Coin and Stamp Fair, being held in Tunbridge Wells, Kent.

Private   1979 Tunbridge Wells Stamp Fair Flowers   18.00   ☐

1979 The Boots Company Limited (9th May)

Issued by The Boots Company Ltd to commemorate the 9th European Congress of Rheumatology.

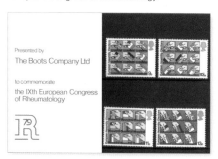

Private   1979 The Boots Company Limited   75.00   ☐

1979 Haddo House (22nd August)

Contains a set of stamps issued to commemorate the Centenary of the death of Sir Rowland Hil.

Private   1979 Haddo House   20.00   ☐

1980 Scottish Wildlife Trust Birds (16th January)

Issued by the Scottish Wildlife Trust, this pack was designed to make children and adults more aware of the nation's wildlife heritage, and the need to protect it.

Private   1980 Scottish Wildlife Trust Birds   15.00   ☐

1980 Daily Mail Ideal Home (3rd March)

This pack was specially produced as a Souvenir of the 1980 Daily Mail Ideal Home Exhibition, held at Earls Court, London, and contains the 1979 Dogs stamps. Other stamp issues were also used in the same pack, at the same event.

Private   1980 Daily Mail Ideal Home   15.00   ☐

1980 Liverpool and Manchester Railway
(12th March)

Commemorating 150 years of the Vulcan Foundry, located in Newton-le-Willows. The pack shows just a little of the history and a few of the locomotives built at the Foundry over the years.

Private   1980 Liverpool and Manchester Railway   80.00   ☐

1981 Penny Collection

Produced by Stanley Gibbons, exclusively for WH Smith and Doubleday Book Clubs, this pack features details of the eight enclosed stamps and Monarchs represented on them.

Private   1981 Penny Collection   20.00   ☐

1981 WIPA Folklore ("Europa") (6th February)

This is one of three presentation packs issued on the occasion of the Internationale Postwertzeichen Ausstellung, held in Vienna from 22nd May to 31st May 1981. They are known as the WIPA packs.

Private   1981 WIPA Folklore ("Europa")   12.50   ☐

1981 Daily Mail Ideal Home (10th March)

This pack was specially produced as a Souvenir of the 1981 Daily Mail Ideal Home Exhibition, held at Earls Court, London, and contains the 1980 London Landmarks stamps. Other stamp issues were also used in the same pack, at the same event.

Private   1981 Daily Mail Ideal Home   15.00   ☐

1981 International Year of the Disabled

(25th March)

This pack was specially produced for The South of England Stamp, Coin and Postcard Fair held on 23rd May 1981. The Fair featured a giant raffle in aid of Guide Dogs for the Blind.

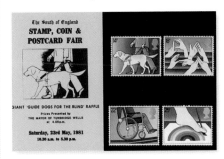

Private   1981 International Year of the Disabled   12.00   ☐

1981 Scottish Wildlife Trust Butterflies (13th May)

Issued by the Scottish Wildlife Trust, this pack was designed to make children and adults more aware of the nation's wildlife heritage, and the need to protect it. (Qty. issued 1,000)

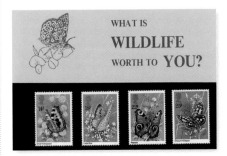

Private   1981 Scottish Wildlife Trust Butterflies   8.50   ☐

1981 WIPA Butterflies (13th May)

This is one of three presentation packs issued on the occasion of the Internationale Postwertzeichen Ausstellung, held in Vienna from 22nd May to 31st May 1981. They are known as the WIPA packs.

Private   1981 WIPA Butterflies   12.50   ☐

1981 WIPA Year of the Disabled (25th May)

This is one of three presentation packs issued on the occasion of the Internationale Postwertzeichen Ausstellung, held in Vienna from 22nd May to 31st May 1981. They are known as the WIPA packs.

| Private | 1981 WIPA Year of the Disabled | 12.50 | ☐ |

1981 South of England Stamp Fair (1st August)

This pack was specially produced for The South of England Stamp, Coin and Postcard Fair held on 1st August 1981, giving it the title 'Lammastide'.

| Private | 1981 South of England Stamp Fair | 20.00 | ☐ |

1982 Covent Garden Stamp Festival (28th April)

This superb design, issued by the Stamp Collecting Promotion Council, shows Covent Garden Theatre illustrated on the outside, with a cardboard cutout 'pop-up' theatre scene of characters on the inside.

| Private | 1982 Covent Garden Stamp Festival | 12.00 | ☐ |

1986 Domesday (17th June)

Commemorating the 900th Anniversary of the Domesday Book, this pack discusses the link between the Book that is a milestone in English history, the Bayeux Tapestry and Halley's Comet, which reappeared in 1986.

| Private | 1986 Domesday | 40.00 | ☐ |

1990 RSPCA (23rd January)

Produced by the RSPCA to commemorate their 150th year, this pack was sent to donors to thank them for their support of the charity.

Private   1990 RSPCA   100.00   ☐

2006 Cancer Research

Produced by Cancer Research UK to raise awareness of the charity and the importance of continued research in the fight to overcome the many different forms of the disease.

Private   2006 Cancer Research   75.00   ☐

2006 The National Assembly Senedd (1st March)

This pack marks the official opening, on St David's Day, of the new Welsh Assembly building, Senedd, and contains photos plus information about the architectural design, building and environmental performance of the structure. Written in English and Welsh.

Private   2006 The National Assembly Senedd   90.00   ☐